I0901940

# ACTS: THE POWER THAT CHANGES THE WORLD

Howard Brown

STUDY GUIDE WITH LEADER'S NOTES

New Growth Press
newgrowthpress.com

New Growth Press, Greensboro, NC 27401
newgrowthpress.com


Cover Design: Dan Stelzer
Interior Typesetting and eBook: Lisa Parnell, lparnellbookservices.com
Exercises and Application Questions: Jack Klumpenhower and Barbara Juliani

ISBN 978-1-64507-440-3 (paperback)
ISBN 978-1-64507-441-0 (ebook)

Printed in India

29 28 27 26 25     3 4 5 6 7

# CONTENTS

# INTRODUCTION

The book of Acts is the story of Jesus—not the Jesus you know from picture books and Sunday school who lived on earth two thousand years ago, but the Jesus you know today who is with you now as he rules from heaven. He's still the same guy, of course. He's every bit the people-noticing, compassion-spilling, bully-fighting, whole-self-giving person he's always been. It's just that now he leads you and loves you from the throne of all power in heaven, and from the right hand of the Father where he whispers how you are the true jewel in his crown.

Acts opens by explaining that it continues the story of Jesus's work begun in the Gospels. It is about his life, and yours, *now*. It is about the Savior who lives for you, and how you get to live for him. He is active today, freeing all kinds of people from their brokenness, conquering dark territories through his sons and daughters who have the Holy Spirit in them to witness everywhere.

By studying this story, you will explore and come to appreciate your place in it. As with the other resources in this series, this study guide will help you do that in a way that keeps your eyes on Jesus, the main character. This means you will also explore and more deeply appreciate all his goodness.

## HOW TO USE THIS STUDY

This study guide is designed to help you learn from Acts within a small group. In Acts, the advancement of God's kingdom—both its expansion in the world and its growth in individual hearts—happens through teams and groups. By meeting as a group, you will draw on this God-in-us power. Make your group a place where people feel free to share what they are learning from God in Acts. Also make it a place where it's safe to still be partly broken, often discouraged, or slow to learn, as many of the people in Acts are.

Each participant should have one of these study guides in order to join in reading and be able to work through the exercises during that part of the study. The study leader should read through both the lesson and the leader's notes in the back of this book before each lesson begins. No other preparation or homework is required. Some parts of Acts will be skipped in this study, and participants might want to read those sections between group meetings, but that won't be necessary to join in the discussions.

There are twelve lessons in this study guide. Each will take about an hour to complete, perhaps a bit more if your group is large, and will include these elements:

**BIG IDEA.** This is a summary of the main point of the lesson.

**BIBLE CONVERSATION.** You will read a passage from Acts and discuss it. As the heading suggests, the Bible conversation questions are intended to spark a conversation rather than generate correct answers. The leader's notes at the back of this book provide some insights, but don't just turn there for the "right answer." At times you may want to see what the notes say, but always try to answer for yourself first by thinking about the Bible passage.

**ARTICLE.** This is the main teaching section of the lesson, written by the book's author.

**DISCUSSION.** The discussion questions following the article will help you apply the teaching to your life.

**EXERCISE.** The exercise is a section you will complete on your own during group time. You can write in the book if that helps you. You will then share some of what you learned with the group.

If the group is large, it may help to split up to share the results of the exercise and to pray, so that everyone has a better opportunity to participate.

**WRAP-UP AND PRAYER.** Prayer is a critical part of the lesson because your spiritual growth will happen through God's work in you, not by your self-effort. You will be asking him to do that good work.

Jesus is bringing the history of the world to a great crest. Look at his work on the earth and in his people! Be amazed, and find your place in that story.

*Lesson*

# 1

# LIFE AFTER JESUS HAS LEFT

## BIG IDEA

Although Jesus is not physically with us today, he gives us real power to make history and work for his kingdom.

## BIBLE CONVERSATION *20 MINUTES*

The events in Acts mark an era of fulfillment. For thousands of years beforehand, the reach and richness of salvation was limited. Old Testament prophets like Joel, who will be quoted in Acts, had told how God's kingdom would someday extend to the whole world and bring his people a fuller life with him. But that message was seldom heard beyond the nation of Israel, which had reached its height of worldly influence under King David and his son Solomon. At the time of Acts, there seemed to be no godly king at all in Israel, only the rule of the Roman Empire and its puppets.

Acts is the second of two volumes written by Luke, a missionary partner of the apostle Paul. In the first, his gospel, Luke tells how Jesus is the greater Son of David who inaugurated the long-awaited kingdom by his birth, ministry, death for sin, and resurrection. But Jesus's kingdom arrives more fully in Acts after he ascends to reign from heaven, beginning the age the Bible calls "the last days." And the kingdom's final fullness is still to come when Jesus returns on "the day of the Lord" to finish defeating death and ridding the world of all evil. With this context in mind, have someone read **Acts 1:1–11** aloud. Then discuss the question below:

Compare service in the kingdom of God, as this passage describes it, with serving a worldly kingdom. What about God's kingdom strikes you as different or amazing, and why?

Chapter 1 goes on tell how the believers, a group of about 120 men and women from all walks of life, picked a twelfth apostle to succeed Judas who had betrayed Jesus. Now skip ahead to **Acts 2:1–21**. Have someone read that passage aloud, or have a few readers take turns, and discuss the two questions below:

If you were one of the visitors to Jerusalem who witnessed this event, what might seem radical or puzzling about it to you? Explain.

Look at the quotation from Joel that Peter uses in verses 17–21, and ask yourself why Peter chose to preach from that passage. What might Peter say is the main thing the crowd should notice about the events they are witnessing?

****

Now read the following article, written by this study guide's author. Take turns reading it aloud, switching readers at each paragraph break. Then discuss the questions that follow the article.

*Lesson*

**1**

**ARTICLE**

# REAL PEOPLE, REAL POWER

*5 MINUTES*

How do you and I act when we have a resurrected Savior who can't be seen anymore? Well, we typically are tempted the way the men and women Jesus left behind must have been tempted. We forget Jesus is a real person with real power. Instead, we spiritualize his acts and promote just another moral philosophy for the world to muse over. Or we create a religion that's a worldly institution, only as powerful as the things we are capable of doing, built on the ideals of a now-gone leader whose dreams we try to keep alive, even if it is just by putting his face on the back of funeral fans and talking about what Jesus would do in this-or-that situation.

But the book of Acts shows a people and a God who, well, *act*. They act unlike anyone else the world has ever known. Acts is God making history, unfolding it with people, power, and his personal involvement. And it is *our* family history if we are believers. It helps us know how we should act and how God is acting in us.

**First, God calls a *people* to make history.** Before Jesus ascended, his disciples were probably expecting him to take out the Roman Empire and the corrupt religious leaders, and be the second coming of King David. But you and I can understand his kingdom more clearly since we see the whole story. Jesus was saying that heaven will come to all the earth. It will impact real people living in real places. It will insert and assert itself in their lives. God intends to drive history.

We need to grasp this, and let it grip us. Christianity, the continuing powerful ministry of Jesus Christ, is about movement. It is about doing things—creating momentum and change and challenge. Jesus's promise of the Holy Spirit means God is going to crash into his people and then through us collide into the world and its ways.

**Second, God gives a *power* to make history.** The 120 believers who were gathered on Pentecost were already followers of Jesus, but they needed powerful life change to testify about him. I say life, because the word *wind* in 2:2 also means "breath" as in new life. The sign of being filled with the Spirit was speaking in earthly, foreign tongues. This world's cultures, economies, and social structures—how people live and speak and *act*—will be changed by God's powerful work.

How can I describe it? My man in verse 13 almost has it right: "They are filled with new wine." It's like being drunk with God's living presence. You see and live things on a God slant. You are just crazed enough to represent *God* on this earth, and to do it with fire. You live in this dark, cold world with light and warmth and comfort and truth.

But the Bible says even the good, devout people in town for Pentecost were bewildered. You see, most of the time God's power is undercover and invisible. The people in the world we are called to impact don't recognize the power as being from God. It looks like foolishness—a bunch of misguided, "flicted" souls. People do not see God's kingdom coming. They do not see how it will infiltrate evil to break and rebuild and heal it. That's because God's power looks like you and me.

It's in regular men, women, children, and community groups, who are cracked and torn and unsure.

**Third, God gives a *Lord* to make history.** Here is the plan: God will use his sons and daughters to tell what they have heard from the Lord Jesus himself, so that from this one group of people every kind of person can be made right from every wrong: every wrong way they've been treated, every wrong way they've treated others, every wrong way they've treated themselves. Jesus's kingdom will be established powerfully among all people.

And you—yes, you who are his—are those sons and daughters. You are the carriers and receivers of prophesy, of God's truth. Verse 18 says, "Even on my male servants and female servants." This means us, raggedy Christians—and there are many of us who are raggedy! Maybe you aren't polished or proper at all, you don't know the right Christian things to say, you can't recite a full Bible verse to save your life, or you don't know if you will feel like a Christian tomorrow or not. Surprise! The Spirit of God has been poured out on and in you.

This is the booming bass beat behind all history. Who is it for? It's for "everyone who calls upon the name of the Lord" (v. 21). We have a living Lord, a resurrected and ascended Savior. Though he is bodily absent, he is spiritually present to love us and walk with us, and he will return to make all things right and put the final beat to history's chatter.

Call on his name. Call him your Lord, and call on him to be the Lord of all. Call on him to be your Redeemer, to guide you through the confusion, and to make all things right. Call on him to change you for the better, to be your provider and protector, and to guard you from the evil one. Call him Jesus, who uses real people in real places by his real power.

## DISCUSSION *10 MINUTES*

How do you tend to forget Jesus's realness or power because you don't see him?

How does it feel to realize that while Jesus is gone, you represent him on the earth?

Lesson 1

EXERCISE

# ORDINARY AND EXTRAORDINARY

*20 MINUTES*

The opening chapters of Acts show how God's plan is to make extraordinary use of ordinary people like you. Not every believer is called to preach publicly or travel the world, but all have power to tell what is true and demonstrate the goodness Jesus is bringing to the earth. For this exercise, you will think about how this applies in your life.

Work through both parts of the exercise on your own, thinking about how you are ordinary but God's power in you is extraordinary. Then when the group is ready, help others get to know you by sharing some of your responses.

**PART 1: How are you ordinary?** The article described believers as raggedy—not naturally people who look like good prospects to help advance Jesus's kingdom. Although God may have already equipped you in many ways to tell about Jesus or show his kindness, how do you still feel naturally ill-equipped or ordinary? Check all that apply.

I feel like **I don't have much** . . .

- ☐ Training/experience in how to serve God
- ☐ Status/clout in the world or my community
- ☐ Bible knowledge
- ☐ Ability to connect with people
- ☐ Compassion for others
- ☐ Time or resources
- ☐ Intimacy with God that keeps me renewed
- ☐ Discipline/progress in godly behavior
- ☐ Other: ______________________________
- ☐ Other: ______________________________

**PART 2: How is God's power in you extraordinary?** Your natural ordinariness is overcome by God's power working in you, so think about that as well. Answer at least one of the questions below:

What is one feature of God's power, seen in Acts 1 and 2, that encourages you despite your natural ordinariness?

______________________________________________

______________________________________________

______________________________________________

What is one way God has worked in or through you that encourages you?

________________________________________

________________________________________

________________________________________

When the group is ready, share and explain some of your results. How are you ordinary? How are you encouraged, and why?

## WRAP-UP AND PRAYER *10 MINUTES*

Use Jesus's Great Commission in Acts 1:8 as a template for your prayer time together. It has two parts:

1. **"You will receive power."** Ask your Father to use your study of Acts to strengthen and renew you as you tap into his Word and pray together.
2. **"You will be my witnesses."** Pray about your involvement in the great mission that marks this era of gospel fulfillment. Ask God to provide opportunities to tell about Jesus and demonstrate the goodness of his kingdom, or to support that work, either individually or as a group.

*Lesson*

# 2

# GOD'S GIFT, THE CHURCH

## BIG IDEA

Gospel preaching gives birth to believers who are no longer isolated individuals, but come together to form a glad, generous, glorious church.

## BIBLE CONVERSATION *20 MINUTES*

So far in Acts, the risen Lord Jesus has ascended to heaven, and the Holy Spirit has come to empower his church. Peter has begun preaching to the curious crowd that gathered, explaining how the Spirit's outpouring marks a worldwide era of salvation for all who believe. Now Peter will continue his sermon by telling the crowd about Jesus, quoting two psalms written by King David. One shows David foretelling how Jesus would rise from the dead, and the other shows David foretelling how Jesus would ascend to reign over all his enemies. Have someone read **Acts 2:22–47** aloud, or have a few readers take turns. Then discuss the two questions below:

Imagine that you, like Peter, were telling a group of your peers why Jesus should matter to them. What does Peter say about Jesus that you would find important to say too?

What might explain why the group of three thousand new believers felt such closeness to each other?

Now skip ahead to **Acts 4:32–35**, which describes the church after thousands more people believed. Have someone read that passage aloud. Then discuss the question below:

What do you find appealing about the church community described in this passage and in chapter 2, and why?

****

Now take turns reading the article aloud, switching readers with each paragraph. When you finish, discuss the questions that follow.

*Lesson*

2

ARTICLE

# THE CHURCH IS A NOUN

*5 MINUTES*

I remember growing up in a neighborhood with many military-officer families. We kids would play military games, shooting our fake rifles from ditches that were our fake bunkers. We had a great time, but then the oldest decided to make it a "thing." He gave us ranks and duties. He even talked about dues and meetings. That was good for about two days, and then the fun was over.

We fear the same thing happening to our Christianity. We worry that it will become an institution and that we will lose our freedom and joy in it. Or we may have been wrongly taught that it is foundationally a personal relationship with God, free like a spirit. We think of church as something we *do* or *feel*, as if it were a verb or adjective instead of a noun—people, in a place, who are a thing.

We also don't trust things that involve obedience and accountability, and for good reason. Leaders abuse, and institutions become cold. As a pastor who has been on both ends of spiritual and institutional abuse, let me say I'm sorry. I hate the way we have sometimes made church membership and submission a burden. I don't blame you for thinking you should keep control of your own, individual, open relationship with God. I understand that many relationships with God have been hurt in the church.

But although it's scary, I must still encourage you to embrace the church and being the church. Acts is teaching us that this is not just our obligation. It is our honor and privilege as those who take the mark and name of Jesus the Christ. We become people who worship him together and receive care. Jesus died and rose, and the Holy Spirit came, to give you the glory that is the church. Don't let it pass you by.

In this passage, we see that by God's design his church is about three things. **The first is *contract*.** The sign of accepting Jesus was submission and commitment to the faith and to the faithful. In the Greek world, you might show your commitment to a benefactor or employer by receiving a mark like a piercing or tattoo. Or your commitment might be to a school or philosophy whose teachers you followed. Also, the people you welcomed into your house and ate with declared deep social commitments.

Acts shows the believers doing all of this. As those contracted through the blood of Jesus to be his, God's people vowed commitment to each other. They bore the common mark of baptism, and they kept the ceremony of belonging—breaking the bread and saying the prayers. They followed their leaders' teaching, and they shared their food and houses with each other. They committed not only to the Lord Jesus, the great benefactor and philosopher of the institution, but to the institution itself. They submitted their identities and lives to it. The Holy Spirit made a noun out of the verb of what God was doing in the hearts of his people.

**Second, this contract calls for necessary *contact*.** It means being in a common place as a common people. "All who believed were together and had all things in common" (2:44). There were no levels of entry or VIP sections. The church was for any who believed in Jesus regardless of money, age, nationality, former religion, class, or ethnicity. Notice how there were no private worship places. It was all about doing the faith together, touching and smelling and seeing each other.

But open-to-all does not mean a free-for-all party. Let's say you are invited to my house. You are welcome to come the way you are. But if you come, you will be called to a common meal of various meats, barbeque sauces, and music that I have chosen. In the same way, church is not about a bunch of individual, personal encounters with God. It is about all of us coming to the same encounter with the same Savior through his common gifts: the bread, the prayers, the teachings, the worship. And we come not with our critiques and preferences, but "with glad and generous hearts" (2:46).

**Third, this is possible because our contact is built on gospel *content*.** The church is a place where God is at work through the message. Look how the whole thing started. Peter got up to preach the gospel. Three thousand people got saved and baptized and joined the church after hearing this message: You are sinners before God. You misunderstood and ignored Jesus. But Jesus died and rose again for you. He came to save you from your sins. He has been gracious and generous to you. He was kicked out of temples and synagogues so you could be in a church, where you get all the grace and power he has for you.

From that gospel message comes gospel mayhem. "They were selling their possessions and belongings and distributing the proceeds to all" (2:45). This is not regular. Don't let anyone tell you it's normal. It only makes sense because the gospel is alive in the hearts of the believers as they vow together, giving and sharing their stuff and their lives, submitting to each other and to the leadership.

This was a miracle. It was the Lord who "added to their number" (2:47). For you too, it may feel like a miracle, given your stories of distrust or spiritual abuse, that you have joined a church or will even gather with a group of believers. But God uses his church as a vortex of love and grace, a tornado of power, to draw us to himself. It is more than a noun; it is many nouns—praise, thanksgiving, sacrament, preaching, teaching, loving, fellowship, gifts, power, addition, and God's very presence as we gather. Don't miss what God has for you in and as the church.

## DISCUSSION *10 MINUTES*

How have you been taught to think of the church? How and why have those thoughts changed?

The article calls the church a gift of glory from God. How can that way of seeing it be helpful to you?

Lesson 2

EXERCISE

# GLAD AND GENEROUS HEARTS

*20 MINUTES*

The description of the believers in Jerusalem is a sign of what results when hearts are "glad and generous" (2:46). For this exercise, you will use that phrase to think about your life with Jesus and his people. On your own, read through each of the prompts below, one for a GLAD heart and the other for a GENEROUS heart. Then write a few words (or draw a simple picture) inside each heart shape to tell how your heart is glad and might be generous. You'll share your responses with the group at the end of the exercise.

**PART 1: Your GLAD heart.** What have you noticed in this lesson's passages that makes you thankful for Jesus? You might be:

- **Glad for the gospel.** Something Peter said about Jesus's saving work makes you especially thankful and glad.
- **Glad for God's work in your life.** Like the believers in Jerusalem were "cut to the heart" (2:37) and had awe come upon them (2:43), you are joyful about some way God has impacted you.

- **Glad for the church.** Something about the descriptions of the Jerusalem church makes you thankful for the church and community of believers God has given you.

Pick <u>one</u>, and write or draw something in the heart below to explain how you are glad.

**My GLAD Heart**

**PART 2: Your GENEROUS heart.** Out of the gladness God has given you, what kind of giving might flow from your heart? You might be eager to be:

- **Generous with your home and possessions.** There's some way you might share your daily life and resources with other believers.
- **Generous with your preferences.** You might let go of certain critical attitudes, worship/ministry preferences, or other individualistic or selfish things you hold tightly at church.
- **Generous with your story.** *Your* story is *our* story as a church, so you might have a way to tell what God has done in your life, invite others to share in your story, or invest in the stories of other believers.

Pick one, and write or draw something in the heart below to explain how you might be generous.

**My GENEROUS Heart**

When the group is ready, share some of your responses. What makes your heart glad, and how are you eager to be generous?

## WRAP-UP AND PRAYER *10 MINUTES*

Your work in creating a glad and generous church community involves partnering with the Holy Spirit, who powers the church. You've done some of that by studying the Spirit-breathed Bible together. Now also pray together, asking God to fill your hearts with gladness and generosity, and to make your church glorious.

*Lesson*

# 3

# ALL THAT JESUS GIVES

## BIG IDEA

Jesus came to heal us from every effect of sin that was hobbling us. We should not settle for less than all that he gives.

## BIBLE CONVERSATION *20 MINUTES*

Acts has described how three thousand people believed in Jesus and joined the church in Jerusalem. Next, the book will recount an event that followed at the temple there. In the Old Testament and up until Jesus's death and resurrection, the temple was God's designated hub for worship of the Lord. It was the place of his presence with his people, and of daily sacrifices, prayers, and teaching. All of this was pointing to the Christ, through whom God had promised to bring forgiveness, renewal, and life in his kingdom.

But the temple was ruled by the Sadducees, elite Jews who aligned with the Roman occupation. They did not believe in some of the most world-changing blessings the Christ would bring, including an end-times resurrection. They had taken the lead in getting Jesus crucified, especially after he told them he was the Christ who would return in glory.* Many of the people of Jerusalem, as well, had settled for being proud temple-goers outwardly while inwardly putting more hope in status and achievement than in the Christ who would come to free them from sin.

A key character in the story is a man born lame who begged at one of the temple gates. The temple rulers were known to despise those born with defects, and their laws at the time may have prohibited the man from entering the temple or some of its courts. In any case, the man would not have been able to climb the temple's many steps. But the prophets and Jesus himself had used the healing and inclusion of the lame as a sign of God's kingdom, with its restorative wholeness, finally arriving.**

Now have someone read **Acts 3:1–4:4** aloud, or have a few readers take turns. Then discuss the account using the questions below:

How is Peter and John's encounter with the lame man different from your typical interaction with beggars? Why might Peter and John act the way they do?

*. For this event and the murderer release Peter will refer to, see Matthew 26:57–68; 27:1–2, 11–26.

**. For example, see Isaiah 35:5–6; Micah 4:6–7; Luke 7:18–23.

Look at what the man did after he was healed. Which of his actions are like what you might do in a similar situation, and which are different? Explain.

Notice how Peter speaks about the whole history of salvation, from long-ago promises to the future heavenly life. How does it help for his listeners, and for you, to appreciate the full story?

****

Now read this lesson's article aloud, taking turns by paragraph, and discuss the questions that follow.

Lesson 3

ARTICLE

# WALK ON IN

*5 MINUTES*

Don't think this is a story about one man who was healed. When Peter and John gave healing to the beggar at the temple gate, they were dispensing something bigger. They were declaring that all of God's chosen people (and yes, its leaders too) were like the crippled man. All were hindered by sin. All were trapped. All were settling for less than God had promised. And all of them, like us today, needed Jesus to heal them in the heart. They needed to be made right with God and fit to come and worship—and in Jesus they could be! They could just walk right in.

We too find ourselves on the outside. We are looking in at the grace and freedom and worship and fellowship that could be ours, but we are hobbled and hindered by sin. Some of it is our own sin: maybe you've tried some crazy things that have left damage on your soul and even in your body. Some of it is the sin of others: you've been hollowed out and counted out and knocked out by evil, so that now you can't walk in what God gives. And some of it is the broken world: you're just beat down by life's problems and sadness.

It all means you live in constant fear of worship, fellowship, and confession of sin. Spiritually, you are crippled by hurt and failure, so that you can't trust the Lord and his people. The guilt and pain and fear that separate you from God have become a part of who you are and how you live. As you are, you cannot just walk on in.

Later in Acts 4, the crowd was astounded at the healing because the man "was more than forty years old" (v. 22). Maybe for you too it's been years. After all this time of being hindered, you figure God is done with you. You've decided you're not the worshipping type. Outside the gate is your place. You've settled there, a lifelong beggar at the temple. In a place and among a people where God is calling you in to be his guest of honor, you've settled for spare-change handouts.

When our brokenness and fears and sins take long to heal, or don't heal the way we think they should, we settle. We decide we'll just try to make the world a better place. Or we find a feel-good church that's comfortable, where we can play our part and get a little handout. We hope to be successful enough, have enough fun, and find enough love to let us avoid really asking God to move against our demons. We hope what's hurting us won't get jostled, because movement hurts when you're in pain. And we don't want people to really see us and our shame.

But Acts says Peter and John directed their gaze at the lame man, and told the man also to look at them. Jesus came, and the gospel is preached, so you can know that God fixes his gaze on you. The point of Peter's sermon is that God sees you—sinful and broken and hurt—and has sent Jesus to suffer for you "that your sins may be blotted out, that times of refreshing may come from the presence of the Lord" (3:19–20). So repent and look at him. Have the courage to believe that God will forgive you of the sins you've done and will free you from the sins done to you. Jesus has come so that you may come on in. Sin will no longer hinder you. Brokenness will no longer have its way with you.

This man was healed for a greater purpose than just being able to walk again. It's easy to read this story as only being about God giving you the healing. But the man leapt and praised God. He didn't go on his own way, but went through the gate and into the temple to finally praise the Lord. His forty years of suffering were allowed by God so that, at the appointed time, his life would be a testimony to God's awesomeness.

Yes, our lives are a mess. We have settled, looking for silver and gold to make us feel better about ourselves, and God has let our lives be broken. But there is a better way. You don't have to settle for anything less than being a sacrifice of praise to God. Despite all your history and all the evil that has held power over you, Jesus can make your life one that leaps.

Or he might simply make you cling, like the man held onto Peter and John. Sometimes God heals us just enough that we can hang on for dear life to the promises of God. Maybe you don't feel you can shout hallelujah, and your life doesn't dance before the Lord. Then cling to the gospel, which tells you that at just the right time Christ came and died for the ungodly, that your Lord Jesus is the Good Shepherd, and that in Christ no power in all creation can separate you from his love. Not your past. Not your mama. Not how your friends left you. Not what was done to you. Not what shameful things you have done. Not what you're addicted to. Not how many times you have left God.

Cling to Christ, not to your own ability and merits. Rise up in "the faith that is through Jesus" (3:16). Regardless of circumstances and sin and struggle, keep coming to him. Come to the ministry of his word and sacraments, and to the fellowship of his church. Come into the presence of the Lord God. By the power of Jesus, just walk on in.

## DISCUSSION *10 MINUTES*

How do you tend to settle for less than the full times of refreshing that come through Jesus?

How is your life a testimony to God's awesomeness, or how might it be?

*Lesson*

3

EXERCISE

# PEOPLE AT THE TEMPLE

*20 MINUTES*

Our passage in Acts gives you an engaging story about real-life people who encountered Peter and John and their preaching. In some ways, these people at the temple are like you. So on your own, read through the descriptions of the characters found in the account from Acts. Pick one or two characters that remind you of yourself—either now or in your past. You don't need to fit the character in every way, just in some way that makes you say, "Ah, I'm like that." Circle, underline, or write notes if it helps, and be prepared to tell who you picked and why. Which person at the temple are you like?

**BEGGAR** (like the lame man before he was healed)

- Has been hurt or damaged
- Feels left out, unwelcome, or unable to come to God
- Is settling for "silver and gold" that looks shiny, but is less than the glory God offers
- Some other way I'm like the beggar: ____________________

  ______________________________________________

**LEAPER** (like the lame man after he was healed)

- Has been noticeably transformed by God, and is doing what once seemed unthinkable
- Is full of praise and joy, eager to come and worship
- Attracts attention in a way that makes people think, *God must be at work in that person*
- Some other way I'm like the leaper: ____________________

______________________________________________

**CLINGER** (like the man when he kept grabbing onto Peter and John)

- Holds on for dear life to Christ and his people
- Is not done after getting immediate problems fixed, but wants more of whatever God gives
- Wants to move beyond people and handouts that just get you through another day, to Christ who gives healing
- Some other way I'm like the clinger: ____________________

______________________________________________

**ONLOOKER** (like one who outwardly was a good temple-goer or was interested in God)

- May be curious about what God is doing, but unsure
- Appears to be at home among God's people, but doesn't deeply know the forgiveness and victory over sin Jesus offers
- Some other way I'm like an onlooker: ____________________

______________________________________________

**BELIEVER** (like one who heard Peter's preaching and believed)

- Has been gripped by the good news of God's word about sin, forgiveness, and the times of refreshing he will bring
- Is numbered among God's people, gladly worshipping and participating in the church community
- Some other way I'm like a believer: ____________________

____________________________________________

**ACCUSER** (like one of the temple leaders who arrested Peter and John)

- Is quicker to find fault with something than to rejoice over what God has done
- Gets annoyed when things in the church don't go "the right way," or when attention goes to someone else
- Some other way I'm like an accuser: ____________________

____________________________________________

When the group is ready, share and explain some of your responses. Which character reminds you of your own life, and how?

Think about change in your life. Which character describes the kind of person you (1) used to be or (2) hope to become?

## WRAP-UP AND PRAYER *10 MINUTES*

If you aren't sure how to pray for each other, you might use the lame man's experience as a guide:

- How do you need to *walk* (basic needs)?
- How might you *leap* (big goals)?
- How might you *cling* (trust God more)?
- How can your life praise God?

FOR NEXT TIME: The next lesson will skip ahead to Acts 5:12–42 and then to Acts 7:51–60. If you want to read the parts in between as part of your study of Acts, read them on your own before the next time you meet.

*Lesson*

# 4

# THE MISSION AND MESSAGE OF LIFE

## BIG IDEA

In Jesus, we are given a life that will not die and makes us powerful witnesses.

## BIBLE CONVERSATION *20 MINUTES*

Earlier, in Acts 4:4, we were told that the number of men who heard the word and believed in Jesus "came to about five thousand." That was not just evidence of the Holy Spirit's power, but also an ominous sign that opposition would arise. The temple leaders who had Jesus put to death now faced losing popular support. At first, they merely threatened the apostles to stop teaching about Jesus, but now in chapter 5 they will try harsher tactics. Have someone read **Acts 5:12–42** aloud, or have a few readers take turns. Then discuss the two questions below:

Think about the temple leaders and what might be happening in their hearts. What attitudes, emotions, or concerns underlie their treatment of the apostles? Explain.

Now think about what drives the apostles' behavior. How is it different from what motivates the temple leaders, or from what often motivates you?

Acts goes on to tell about a church leader named Stephen. His ministry was so effective he was seized, charged by false witnesses with blasphemy, and put on trial before the council that had condemned Jesus. Stephen preached to the council about God's history of speaking to his people, and how the people and their leaders often rejected God's message. Have someone read aloud how Stephen's sermon ended in **Acts 7:51–60**. Then discuss the final question below:

Which aspects of Stephen's witness and death do you most admire, or which would you like to be true for you as well? Explain.

****

Next, take turns by paragraph reading the article aloud. When you finish, discuss the questions that follow.

Lesson

ARTICLE 4

# THE LIVING DEATH OF JESUS CHRIST

*5 MINUTES*

Jesus's cross reveals something we don't want to see. Our sin, both mine and yours, has murderous results. Our lack of belief, our arrogance about doing things our way, and our fear of no longer being in charge of our lives all require Jesus to be dead to us. They say to crucify him.

The temple leaders, in their pride and fear and jealousy, needed to kill off Jesus. They missed the message that in fact Jesus's death brings relief from those burdens. When you and I cry out to Jesus, our guilt falls on him. We exchange our load of fears for his forgiveness and freedom. We no longer need to hide the ways we are wrong, because we have Jesus and he is right. When we were dead in our sins, he died for us. Now something—no, some*one*—is alive in us.

The temple leaders must have thought the apostles were like the walking dead in a zombie movie. They've been bitten, and now they're infected by a death that won't die. You beat them and they just keep coming. You lock them up, and still they keep following the dead man Jesus. In Stephen's case, even in the face of his own death he won't shut down and shut up.

But what if the teacher Gamaliel was correct? What if the apostles weren't the movie kind of walking dead, but were powered by the living Christ who can't be taken? What if Peter was right in verse 32, and the infection they were given was the Holy Spirit? Then they would walk in a new ability to do what God wants. They would give their bodies, and their whole selves, not to bring death but to spread life.

If you are infected with Jesus, my message to you is *don't fight it*. Jesus is alive. The Holy Spirit in you is real. He will not stop in you, and you will not stop him. The Spirit will give glory and speak praise and give honor to Christ, even if God has to break your life apart to keep the strain of the gospel alive in your body. So give in, and see your calling in this world to be a carrier of the viral love of God's grace.

I know it's scary to stop holding your beliefs to yourself and be open about your faith. Some people will think you are spreading death, lost in a church world that ought to be long-gone and buried. And it will feel like death to you too—death to your complacency and cushy lifestyle. But you have to be willing to walk in death for Jesus, and be marginalized and called a little crazy, to know how alive he is. When you do, the Holy Spirit's power will open prisons and heal sick people around you—mentally, socially, and physically.

And when this life of dying is hard, you can have great hope in the message and the mission of Jesus Christ. This is because the majesty of Jesus lives beyond death, and he rules over death. As Stephen was about to be stoned, he let the temple leaders know that he saw what Peter and John had declared: Jesus is alive, and he is standing at the right hand of God. The right hand means Jesus is judge and ruler. He was ruling over Stephen's stoning and over those stoning him. He was watching and judging, and he keeps an account of every wrong done to his people—who belong to him both in life and in death.

Jesus's resurrection was more than just getting up from death. He rose to ascend to his coronation as Leader and Savior. When the temple leaders killed him, they had helped to usher the Son of Man to his throne in heaven. So, if you are living in stubborn opposition or apathy toward Jesus, understand that you are not opposing me, or the church, or the tradition, or a philosophy you disagree with. You are living against the King of kings. This passage is a call to stop fighting the Lord's rule. Rest yourself, and be overcome. Be taken, for the good of your soul.

And if you are trusting Jesus but you are suffering in this world, pushing against pain, being ridiculed by others or even on the inside by your own voice, know that Jesus is not just sitting around. He stands up for you in your suffering. He has your back, even in death. And he lives to return the dead to life. Stephen knew this when he prayed, "Lord Jesus, receive my spirit" (7:59).

Beyond the resurrection of Jesus, there is the resurrection of all who believe in him. The grave will not be the end for you and me. Our perfected souls will meet up with perfected bodies, under a perfect Leader on a perfect world. All that has troubled us and pained us and stolen from us will be left in the grave, and life will take hold of us. It will not be some sort of impersonal-force zombie life, but the life of God that defeats all corruption.

This is why Peter and John and Stephen and all those thousands of believers came to Jesus despite death and hardship. They came because one day Jesus will break the sky open and give us a call: "Get up! You of troubled minds and damaged souls, guilty of much against me, get up! Condemnation will not have you; I will! Sin and death will not have you; I will! Get up and be made whole." And we will rise as he did that first resurrection Sunday. Today we live, and we die, for that day.

## DISCUSSION *10 MINUTES*

The article says being open about your faith or stepping out to serve Jesus will mean dying to yourself. When has doing those things felt like death to you?

The article also says Jesus's forgiveness brings relief from jealousy and from the fear of what people think. When have you felt that to be true for you?

Lesson 4 EXERCISE

# GAZING INTO HEAVEN

*20 MINUTES*

Because Stephen's gaze into heaven is recorded for you in Acts, it is an opportunity for you too to look at Jesus in his glory and be encouraged. Notice what Stephen saw when the heavens were opened for him:

- Stephen saw that Jesus is **alive**.
- Stephen saw that Jesus is **ascended** to heaven.
- Stephen saw that Jesus is **at God's right hand**. This signifies Jesus's headship of the church and his power over the world, and is a position of honor and favor.
- Stephen saw that Jesus is **returning**. The wording that says Stephen "gazed into heaven" recalls the apostles in Acts 1:10–11 who were "gazing into heaven" to try to see Jesus as the angels assured them that he would return.

On your own, read through the list of ways those truths about Jesus are an encouragement to you if you belong to him.[1] From the list, pick <u>one</u> bulleted item that is especially meaningful to you, or one you want to think about further. Read the Bible passage that goes with that item, and spend a few minutes contemplating it. Be ready to share what you learn from the passage or appreciate about it.

**Because Jesus is ALIVE, risen from the dead . . .**

- You can be sure that the deadly punishment for your sin is finished. Jesus has completely paid your penalty, and God has fully accepted his payment, declaring that Jesus did not deserve to die but instead died for you. **READ: Psalm 103:1–4.**
- Sin and death are conquered by your Savior who is alive today, living for you. He will complete his conquest of sin and death in your life. **READ: Romans 6:8–11.**
- You too have passed from the realm of death into eternal life. You are spiritually alive, and your body will rise from the grave as well, resplendent and unkillable. **READ: John 5:24–26.**

**Because Jesus is ASCENDED to his throne in heaven . . .**

- He bestows on you his kingly gifts and power, sending the Holy Spirit, equipping you to spread his fame and message of salvation throughout the world, and blessing you with all that is good. **READ: Psalm 68:32–35.**
- You are assured that you too will gain all the riches of the heavenly life, since you are destined to be with Jesus. **READ: John 14:1–3.**
- You are reminded to keep your focus on the blessings and values of heaven, where your loving Savior is. **READ: Colossians 3:1–4.**

**Because Jesus is AT GOD'S RIGHT HAND, holding honor and power . . .**

- Whatever you experience in the church, and whatever evils surround you in the world, you can know that Jesus is the true leader of his people and the ruler of every king. He will defend you against his enemies, purify his church, and work all things for your good. **READ: Ephesians 1:19–23.**

- You too are seated with Jesus in the heavenly places (Ephesians 2:6), which means you too are a delight to God and not a disappointment. You are beautiful in his eyes, and a shining jewel in the world. **READ: Isaiah 62:2–4.**

**Because Jesus is RETURNING to judge evil and restore the world . . .**

- You are assured that evildoers who hurt you today will bow before Jesus tomorrow, and you will be vindicated. **READ: Philippians 3:18–21.**
- Your work for Jesus's kingdom will have lasting value in a restored world freed from evil and death, and you will inherit your place of honor as a son or daughter of God. **READ: Romans 8:20–23.**

When the group is ready, tell which item you picked and why. What did you appreciate in the Bible passage or learn from it?

How might that truth about Jesus encourage you when being a witness for him or serving his kingdom is hard?

## WRAP-UP AND PRAYER *10 MINUTES*

Pray together that the vision Stephen had of Jesus would sink into you, making you witnesses for Jesus and workers for his kingdom.

FOR NEXT TIME: The next lesson will skip ahead to Acts 9. If you want to read the section in between as part of your study of Acts, read chapter 8 on your own before the next time you meet.

*Lesson*

# 5

# LIGHT AND LIFE

## BIG IDEA

We need Jesus to take us through darkness so that he can bring us into his light, his love, and give us new his new life.

## BIBLE CONVERSATION *20 MINUTES*

Following Stephen's martyrdom at the end of Acts 7, the believers in Jerusalem began to suffer violent persecution. Leading the attack was a young man named Saul who would become the apostle called Paul. Saul had approved of Stephen's execution. "Saul was ravaging the church, and entering house after house, he dragged off men and women and committed them to prison" (8:3). The believers fled Jerusalem, scattering to the coast or northward to places like Samaria, Damascus, and Antioch where the Jewish leadership had lesser influence. But as the believers spread out, they also told about Jesus everywhere, and many who heard believed. Jesus's statement about the gospel spreading "in Jerusalem and in all Judea and Samaria, and to the end of the earth" (1:8) was beginning to come true.

As for Saul, the Bible tells us he was born in the intellectual city of Tarsus, raised in Jerusalem, and educated under the respected Jewish teacher Gamaliel. He became a strict Pharisee, rigorously keeping the

Bible's laws.[*] This gave Saul flawless credentials in the Jewish world and a bright-looking future, so that what happened next is one of the Bible's most impactful conversion stories. Have someone read **Acts 9:1–31** aloud, or have a few readers take turns. Then discuss the following questions:

Compare what Saul was like as a person before he encountered Jesus with who he was afterward. What changes do you notice in him, and how well can you relate to him?

Next, consider the world *around* Saul—his relationships, work, physical surroundings, etc. What changes did he have to navigate, and how well do you relate?

Now look at what Jesus does and says in this account. What do you notice about him that makes him worthy of worship and lifelong service?

****

Now take turns reading the article aloud, switching readers with each new paragraph. Then discuss the questions that follow.

---

*. See Acts 22:3–5; Galatians 1:13–14; Philippians 3:4–6.

*Lesson*

**5**

**ARTICLE**

# KNOCKED DOWN BY JESUS

*5 MINUTES*

Once when I was in sixth grade, I went to the house of a kid named Troy to play football. It became about who was the new top kid on the block. Troy was smaller and I had something to prove, so I was pushing and mistreating him during football. He tried not to get into it, until one more shove from me pushed him over the edge. *So you want to fight, do you?* He put a boxing move on me, and when his fist connected with my eye it was so hard it was like a flashing light. In that split second, I had enlightenment. My dazed mind realized I was going to get my behind kicked—and then everything went black. I was enlightened and I was disabled by darkness all at the same time.

That's what happened to Saul. He was picking a fight with Jesus, and Christ knocked him into a new life of darkness. Of course, Saul had been living in darkness already but didn't know it. He was Bible-educated, Greek-educated, sure in his beliefs, and righteous in keeping the commandments of God. But the brightness of his own ability made him blind about his life.

When Saul retells the story of his conversion later in Acts, he adds that Jesus told him, "It is hard for you to kick against the goads"

(Acts 26:14). A goad is used to poke cattle and get them moving in the right direction. Saul was so sure and arrogant it was like he was hitting electric fences in his life and decided to keep going. His own teacher, Gamaliel, had said to leave the Christians alone. *You might be opposing God.* But Saul's sense of truth wouldn't let him listen to someone wiser. He was bringing death on others in the name of God, acting like God's savior instead of someone saved by God. He was so consumed with how he was right that he had gone wrong.

If you and I are living in our own light, apart from Jesus, we will become blind to the truth. We will become ignorant and self-destructive and murderous in pursuing our own sense of right and wrong. We may think ourselves "right" in many ways: right in how we quote the Bible, right in how successful we are, right in how moral we are, right in how loved and respected we are. But our arrogance will begin to hurt those we are called to help—our spouses, our kids, our churches, our communities. This happens whether we are non-believers who have yet to trust Jesus or believers who will not trust him with some area of our lives.

Before we go too far down the road of our righteous crusade, we might want to realize it is only by Christ that we will see the light—and it will not always feel good. Jesus will throw punches that feel like cheap shots. He will make all we love and hope for crumble. He will make all we lean on and think is true fade into darkness. He will make us like Saul, eyes open but unable to see, left with Jesus alone to trust for light. That's what true conversion and faith can feel like.

It's scary, losing the self-created righteousness you used to have, letting Jesus take all you've believed and lived and been afraid to live. On your own you would never give it up; Jesus needs to knock you down. Every believer has first been left dazed. And you grow in a similar fashion: Jesus continues to show up and knock you down in his grace to bring you back when you wander.

But Jesus does not leave you in the dark or alone. He knows that when you come to trust him, or to trust him more deeply, former friends may become enemies. It might be hard to trust the church, or for people in the church to trust you. You may think you have been too bad for Jesus to love you. You may feel the things you are turning from are too much for the church to handle. But Jesus has given you his people to come into your life.

Notice how Jesus stayed with Saul, but did so through Ananias: "Brother Saul, the Lord Jesus who appeared to you on the road by which you came has sent me" (9:17). Later, the disciples helped Saul escape Damascus. Then Barnabas took him to the apostles. Finally, the brothers in Jerusalem brought him safely out of that city. Through his words and his sacraments and his community, Jesus holds you in and helps you get past all the wrong you have done. *He* refuses to leave you or lose you.

So push past the fear. Like Saul, be obedient and walk toward the church. Give your life to Jesus and receive his care from his people. Saul was a killer who hated the Lord, and Jesus could have—*should* have in the minds of many—knocked him to his death and sent him to hell. But the Lord is unbelievable. He does not punish those he has called to be his. You have persecuted him and kicked against him, and he loves you anyway with a love that is so extravagant, it is almost unbelievable.

Now he calls you to an unbelievable life. You will be able to love like you couldn't before. You will be willing to suffer like you wouldn't before. You will be bold to tell others about Jesus like you haven't before. You will be able to say no to things you couldn't live without before. He may use you to reach your sphere of influence, like science or education or business, in ways you can't imagine. Your marriage and your friendships and your children and your money will go and do unbelievable things, as you walk in the light and life of Jesus Christ.

## DISCUSSION *10 MINUTES*

What things about yourself can make you feel you are right when you could be trusting Jesus instead?

When in your life have you "kicked against the goads," resisting ways God was prodding you?

*Lesson*

# 5 EXERCISE

# UNBELIEVABLE LOVE, UNBELIEVABLE LIFE

*20 MINUTES*

The article ended with two truths for every believer: (1) Jesus loves you with an unbelievable love, and (2) Jesus calls you to an unbelievable life. In this exercise, work on your own to think about how those two truths fit together for you. Imagine them as a set of two eyes—for two things Saul saw after his encounter with Jesus.

The eye on the left side of the page is for the **unbelievable love** Jesus has shown you, like he showed Saul. Even if you don't have a dramatic conversion story like that one, there are times you have kicked against Jesus or hurt his people and he has loved you anyway. Beneath the eye on that side, write a brief note about how this has been true for you.

The eye on the right side is for the **unbelievable life** Jesus calls you to. He said of Saul, "I will show him how much he must suffer for the sake of my name" (v. 16). How might your life be like Saul's calling? When you think about ways to tell about Jesus, or places to do it, or people who might hear, what possibilities get you excited? How might you influence people or display Christ's kingdom in the world? How might Jesus empower you to say no to your past, to sacrifice for him, or to suffer? Imagine something that sounds unbelievable, and write a brief note beneath that eye.

The **unbelievable love** Jesus has for me

The **unbelievable life** Jesus calls me to

When the group is ready, discuss some of your responses. What did you put beneath each eye?

Also think about how the two "eyes" work together in one connected life. How might Jesus's **unbelievable love** for you compel you into the unbelievable life you imagine, or sustain you while you live it? And how might the **unbelievable life** you imagine require you to draw ever nearer to the love of Jesus?

## WRAP-UP AND PRAYER *10 MINUTES*

Like Saul, spend some time praying. Thank your Father for his love for you, and ask him to guide your life.

FOR NEXT TIME: The next lesson will skip ahead to the start of Acts 10. If you want to read the section in between as part of your study, read Acts 9:32–43 on your own before the next time you meet.

*Lesson*

# 6

# CROSSING BOUNDARIES

## BIG IDEA

A growing view of the gospel, and of God's work in all kinds of people all over the world, makes us excellent witnesses who cross boundaries for Jesus.

## BIBLE CONVERSATION *20 MINUTES*

Following the conversion of Saul, Acts returns to the ministry of Peter. Like the other apostles, Peter was an observant Jew. The Bible commanded the Jews, as God's holy people, to separate themselves from the surrounding nations who had often led them into evil. Alongside this spiritual cleanliness were ceremonial laws that displayed it outwardly, such as restrictions on eating the many animals God said were unclean for his people. In Peter's day, additional rules took this principle further, so that a Jew would not eat with a Gentile or even enter his house. Rather, he kept himself clean while awaiting the Messiah who would bring true spiritual purity, sweep oppressors from the land, and someday even bring the nations back to God.

Chapter 10 will also introduce us to Cornelius, a Roman military officer and God-fearing Gentile. Outsiders sometimes became Jews, being circumcised and submitting to the law. This allowed Gentiles, who had been alienated from God since the early pages of the Bible, to come into his family. But Cornelius had not taken that step. He was still part of the unclean nations, and a representative of Israel's oppressors on top of that.

Acts has been hinting that Jesus's kingdom will expand to include the nations (*Gentiles* and *nations* are the same Greek word in Acts), and the church was wrestling with this. Chapter 11 will mention the circumcision party, a faction of believers in Jerusalem who insisted that new Gentile converts submit to the Jewish law as they came to Christ. But now God himself will speak on the issue. Have someone read **Acts 10:1–11:18** aloud, or have some readers take turns. Then discuss the questions below:

Look at how God prepared Cornelius and Peter for the moment they would meet. What did he say to these men that you would find helpful in that situation? Explain.

Now look at what happened when the two men met. Which of their actions, attitudes, and words do you appreciate, and why?

Finally, look at the responses other believers had to God's work at Cornelius's house. What do you like about how they responded, or what surprises you?

****

Next, read aloud the article for this lesson, taking turns by paragraph. Discuss the questions at the end of the article when you finish.

*Lesson*

**ARTICLE** 6

# THEM TOO? US TOO?

*5 MINUTES*

Who is best qualified for salvation? And what kind of people make the best Christians? Where I live, we struggle with these kinds of questions. We may be bent toward thinking of one religious or ethnic heritage as the front door—the way into the church and the path to revival. Or the way history has rolled out in my country, with slavery and subordination and unfair wages dividing us, we see oppressors and those oppressed, and we wonder who has fooled themselves into thinking they are the Lord's people. Can they behave like *that*, and gratify *that* lifestyle, and then really be the face and people of God?

But in the conversion of Cornelius, God was showing his church and us that anyone can come to faith. *Anyone*. This is because the Lord himself directs our hearts. He had already made Cornelius "a devout man" (10:2). Then both Cornelius and Peter had visions from God that made their hearts ready to welcome each other. The Lord prepared them and called them to that moment. When Peter stepped into Cornelius's house, he crossed an impossible boundary that could only be removed by the Lord who softens hearts and twists lives.

Regardless of where you are, spiritually or in the circumstances of life, the Lord can direct you too. My own path runs through some strange places: through charismatic-power stuff, through white-evangelical stuff, through trips to do prison ministry, and through an inner-city, black-led, highly seminary-trained Bible study at a Reformed charismatic church that met in an old cigar factory in Charleston, South Carolina. But through hard times and halfway-spiritual things and half-good and half-bad decisions I made, the Lord began to show me the anywhere and anyone of the gospel. Today I'm a church planter in black suburban Atlanta.

Through what you and I may see as random events, the Lord builds roads into the most remote places of people's hearts. By the power of his choice, he blew a tunnel into the hearts of the Gentiles in Cornelius's house, and they believed in Jesus. And the Jews who saw it were blown away too. They had believed God would only give Jesus and his Spirit to those who first became Jews. Weren't the festivals and ceremonial laws the front door to God? Now he was letting folk come in the side door and the back door and through the window too.

Such powerful saving work of God led to impromptu worship. The Gentiles were "speaking in tongues and extolling God" (10:46). And after Peter explained to the council in Jerusalem, they "glorified God, saying, 'Then to the Gentiles also God has granted repentance that leads to life'" (11:18). God had tunneled into them too. He gave them an expanded understanding of the gospel, adding a few more lanes to their narrow-road view of what he was doing through Jesus.

Romans 1:16 says the gospel is "the power of God for salvation to everyone who believes, to the Jew first and also to the Greek." God has chosen to make a way for all people, an onramp from wherever they are: for the oppressed and the oppressors, for the insiders and the outsiders, for those with a good denominational background and those with a bad one. Whatever nation or station they may be in, it cannot stop God's power to reach whom he wants to reach.

God is not prejudiced about you because you are right wing or left wing, or because you homeschool or go to public school, or because you shout in church to show your devotion or keep quiet to show your reverence, or because you're a God-fearing patriot or an anti-establishment type like Jesus. No, God is far more prejudiced than that! He only wants people who come by faith in Christ alone. He is prejudiced to love you by no righteousness of your own. He will declare you clean only because of Jesus. His prejudice is for your life to become a testimony of his grace, and nothing else.

Did you notice the testimonies in Acts 10 and 11? When Peter first shows up, Cornelius shares about God's work in him and what God spoke to him: "Cornelius, your prayer has been heard and your alms have been remembered before God" (10:31). Peter's response is to tell how God has helped him grow in his understanding of what the gospel is all about: "Truly I understand that God shows no partiality" (10:34). Later Peter testifies for the council and they too understand that by faith in Christ alone we are saved. Simply telling what the Lord has done, both for us and in us, helps others keep believing that the gospel is true.

And that gospel story is central to our testimony and to all we do. Acts says that when Peter got to Cornelius's house, he "opened his mouth" (10:34) and out came the gospel. Peter preached the good news of peace that Jesus is Lord. He told how Jesus came, and lived, and died, and rose, and how "everyone who believes in him receives forgiveness of sins through his name" (v. 43).

That's when "the Holy Spirit fell on all who heard the word" (v. 44). This gospel message, wrapped and folded into everything we do, is the power of God to save people and to change you. Your right standing with God gives you the courage to talk about what God is doing in you. It gives you the ability to tell your neighbor about your faith regardless of how messed up your life has been—or is now. It gives you the power to love and care for people who are different from you. This message, that we are sinners and Jesus is a Savior of sinners, changes everything for every kind of person.

## DISCUSSION *10 MINUTES*

What strange places has God taken you to that softened your heart? Explain.

The article says God wants your life to become a testimony to his grace and nothing else. How is your testimony becoming less about you and more about Christ alone? Or how do you want it to change that way?

*Lesson* 6

EXERCISE

# A BIGGER VIEW

*20 MINUTES*

Peter, Cornelius, their friends, and the church in Jerusalem all grew in their understanding of how big God's work is in this era of history. Your view can grow as well. On your own, read through each item below. Pick a few of them (you don't have to do them all) where you see room for growth. Finish the statements about how your sense of God's work is limited and how it might expand. Then discuss the questions at the end.

**A bigger view of WHO'S INCLUDED.** Peter and the Jewish believers began to see Gentile believers as family members. Rather than thinking of them as different, they saw what they had in common—the same Father, the same Spirit, the same baptism, and shared homes and meals. How might you feel more that way about people the world labels as different from you?

| I tend to limit how I think of God's people, those with whom I have much in common, to people who . . . | I could expand my sense of those with whom I have much in common to include . . . |
|---|---|

| **A bigger view of THE GOSPEL MESSAGE ABOUT JESUS.** Cornelius and the Gentiles at his house heard a sermon that revealed how amazing Jesus is and how fully he saves his people. What do you see in Peter's sermon (10:36–43) that expands on how you typically think about Jesus and what he does to save you? | |
|---|---|
| I tend to limit how I think of Jesus and what he does to save me. Often, I only consider how he . . . | I could expand my view of the kind of person Jesus is, and all that he gives me, to include . . . |

| **A bigger view of THE HOLY SPIRIT'S WORK IN PEOPLE.** Peter and the Jewish believers saw indisputable evidence of the Spirit's power to (1) work faith through gospel preaching and (2) change people so that their lives glorify God. How could your confidence in the Spirit's power grow? | |
|---|---|
| I tend to limit my expectations of what the Holy Spirit might do in someone (or in me). I expect only . . . | I could expand my hope in the Holy Spirit's transforming work to include . . . |

**A bigger view of GOD'S PLAN FOR THE NATIONS.** Peter and the leaders in Jerusalem praised God when they saw how he was beginning to fulfill his promise to extend salvation to the nations. How might you grow in excitement for God's mission to bring people from all nations to Jesus?

| I tend to limit how I think of God's agenda to what's happening in . . . | I could expand my view of God's plan for the world to include . . . |
|---|---|

**A bigger view of GODLY HERITAGE.** Peter heard how the Lord honored Cornelius's prayers and fear of the true God, using them to bring many to faith in Jesus and to expand the gospel's reach. How might you better appreciate how God works through heritages and traditions different from your own?

| When I think of God bringing renewal and expanding his kingdom, I think of it coming through believers whose tradition is . . . | I could expand my vision to see how God might be using unexpected heritages like . . . |
|---|---|

When the group is ready, share some of your responses. How is your view of God's work limited, and how might it expand?

Peter crossed into Cornelius's house, and Cornelius crossed through the water of baptism into the church. What about you? With a bigger view of the gospel and God's work in people, what physical boundaries might *you* cross?

## WRAP-UP AND PRAYER *10 MINUTES*

Pray together for God to enlarge your view of his kingdom, his people, and his work in them.

FOR NEXT TIME: The next lesson will skip ahead to Acts 15. On your own, you might want to read the intervening chapters before the next time your group meets. They continue telling Peter's story and describe the start of Paul's missionary work.

Lesson

# 7

# DEFENDING THE GOSPEL

## BIG IDEA

Keeping God's law is a joyful response to his love for us, not a burden by which we or others must earn God's love.

## BIBLE CONVERSATION *20 MINUTES*

At Cornelius's house, the Holy Spirit had shown that God was ending the division between Gentiles and Jews. Although the Jews had rituals of separateness and purity that were part of the biblical law of Moses, this new unity of Jews and Gentiles in Christ did not mean God's people would stop their holy living. On the contrary, the death and resurrection of Jesus confirmed forgiveness and new life, and the outpouring of the Spirit meant God's people would be holier than ever—and found in every nation. They would be empowered to keep God's moral law and stand out from the world in ways far beyond outward rituals. Jesus's kingdom expands obedience, never shrinks it.

Acts 13 and 14 tell how Jesus's former enemy Saul, now called by the Greek name Paul, began taking the gospel into Gentile regions that were also home to some Jews. Along with Barnabas, Paul preached in Cyprus and Galatia where "a great number of both Jews and Greeks believed" (14:1). But when Paul and Barnabas returned, they found that a question had not been settled: Should the Gentile believers now follow the separation and purity rules of the Jews, including the initiation rite of circumcision?

Chapter 15 will mention Jewish believers who were once Pharisees. Pharisees were highly regarded for their careful devotion to all the law of Moses, but Jesus had sparred with them over how their emphasis on outward obedience led to self-righteousness. In Acts, the apostles will not spell out precisely which commands no longer apply in the age of Gentile inclusion, but instead will address the larger matter of whether there's any salvation at all in law keeping. Have someone read **Acts 15:1–32** aloud, or have a few readers take turns. Then discuss the questions below:

On the surface, the dispute in Acts 15 is about Jewish rites. But what deeper concerns or impulses do you suspect each side might have?

Look at how the dispute was resolved. How does it compare to ways you've seen other church disputes ended?

What does James do for the Gentile believers that would feel spiritually caring if he did it for you? Explain what you would appreciate about his actions.

****

Now take turns by paragraph reading the article aloud. Then discuss the questions that follow.

*Lesson*

7

ARTICLE

# THE BREAD-PUDDING CHURCH

*5 MINUTES*

The Jews from Judea were teaching that to become part of the promise of Jesus meant first becoming Jews and being obedient to Jewish religious law. Well, that might sound good. God's law is an expression of his love for his people, right? Obedience is good, and good for us, isn't it? But Paul and Barnabas rightly saw that the Jews' insistence was not actually a call to holiness. It was not even a call to Jewishness, really, nor about which old ceremonies to retain. No, at its heart it was a distortion of Christianity. It was an attack on the gospel itself, which is that we are saved through faith in Christ alone.

This kind of demand and debate still rages in the church today. We wonder if we have done all we must to be saved—or if *that person* has. And this event in Acts teaches us to lean on God's promise that he guides, accepts, and unites his people *by his grace*. The Jews had seen God do miraculous things and had received many blessings. They also had suffered from God's discipline when they didn't obey. So it is no surprise that when Jesus the promised Messiah came, some Jews felt it was a reward from God for following his rules and keeping the ceremonies. They thought that's what brought God to your side.

But look what Peter tells his fellow Jews about the Gentiles: "God, who knows the heart, bore witness to them, by giving them the Holy Spirit just as he did to us, and he made no distinction between us and them, having cleansed their hearts by faith. Now, therefore, why are you putting God to the test by placing a yoke on the neck of the disciples that neither our fathers nor we have been able to bear? But we believe that we will be saved through the grace of the Lord Jesus, just as they will" (vv. 8–11).

Did you get that? God has never accepted his people *because* they expressed their faith rightly or obeyed well enough. The Jews were never perfect enough for God to love them and keep them. Their history is filled with how they worshipped all sorts of idols and doubted the Lord. But God loved them and chose them despite much failure.

Our obedience and expressions of faith are a reaction to what is already true. God has already expressed unconditional love for his people who do not deserve it, who don't worship well enough, who didn't praise him often enough, and who don't do enough of the right things. Peter is saying God was faithful to his people even when they weren't faithful. That's what God's acceptance of us is all about—and we should treat others with the same kind of thinking.

As a father, I don't give my children rules so the kids can earn my love or make me want to keep them. I have already chosen to have them and love them. The obedience is for their good, but it is always about my love for them outside of the rules, outside of their ability to do what I say, outside of how they perform for me or respond to me. Nothing they do could make them no longer loved by me.

In the same way, you and I have not responded well enough to what God has done for us that we should think God accepts us because of our religious expression or good behavior, or impose that on other people. We are too evil and inconsistent in our own mess. We may call people to one thing only: that if you believe, you will be saved regardless of what you have or have not done—through the grace of the Lord Jesus. He lived and died and rose *first*, to lead you to repentance and to deep and loving expressions of faith. In Acts, this gospel message caused the Jews to humble themselves. Nobody won the argument; instead, they became one.

As a kid, one of my favorite things my mom would make was bread pudding. I don't mean the fancy stuff, but a poor man's dessert. Mom would look in the refrigerator and freezer and on the counter, and she would find all sorts of bread. Some was new and soft and sweet from that morning's breakfast. Some was old and hard and forgotten, and even a little moldy. She would take it all and pour cream on it, and add some eggs. She would carefully mush it up until it became a bread sludge, from what was once a slice of this or that. She would then add some raisins in it or maybe some fruit cocktail, and add sugar or cinnamon and put it under the heat of the oven and out came bread pudding—one thing made from many, delicious and pleasing. It had been changed by the hands of a master chef and redeemer.

Every person comes into the church soft or hard, with much history. But God pours in his Spirit. He takes people who were divided over politics, parenting, schools, class, ethnicity, and moral values. Then he mashes them together in the gospel that we are saved by grace through faith in Christ alone. He adds the free gifts of his grace and puts them under the heat of struggle, and out comes a new church and a new oneness, a sweet way of living to the glory of God.

## DISCUSSION *10 MINUTES*

How hard is it for you to believe that God really loves you as his child despite your sins and failures?

How does a deep awareness that we are saved only by God's grace keep you from being pushy (or pushed around) with fellow believers?

*Lesson*

7

EXERCISE

# FALSE SOURCES OF RIGHTEOUSNESS

*20 MINUTES*

Paul wrote to the Gentile churches in Galatia about the conflict in Acts 15. In his letter, he says that even though Jews like himself knew much about God and had much practice in holy living, none of that was enough to save anyone. "We know that a person is not justified by works of the law but through faith in Jesus Christ, so we also have believed in Christ Jesus, in order to be justified by faith in Christ and not by works of the law" (Galatians 2:16).

**Justification** is God's legal declaration that he forgives your sin and counts you righteous. It is a comfort to know that your salvation lies only in Jesus. *He* is righteous enough. When you are joined to him by faith, you too are righteous in God's eyes even though you sin. You can rest, knowing you don't need to earn any part of your salvation by your good behavior or ability to conjure up godliness. Your obedience to God is not *how* you are saved, but is a resulting lifestyle *because* you are saved. Set free from sin, you get to practice holiness.

But even if you know this, it's hard to deeply live out of your justification. Your heart will manufacture some other status, or some rule or performance, that takes Jesus's place and makes you feel acceptable. Usually these are good things, but your heart treats them wrongly. You trust them instead of trusting the righteousness you have in Jesus. They make you feel secure with God or superior to others—or insecure and inferior. To uncover these false sources of righteousness, work through each step of the exercise on your own and then discuss it.

**STEP 1:** Read the list below of things other than Christ alone that might make you feel acceptable or loveable in God's eyes. All of them are good things (or they can be). But check the box next to those your heart uses to make you think God accepts or rejects you. You can also add your own item to any category.

### False Sources of Righteousness

**Godly Behavior**

☐ Level of success in battling certain sins

☐ Track record of fulfilling godly duties

☐ Diligence in following certain commands

☐ Willingness to love others in some way

**Religious Expression**

☐ Amount of vocalness during worship, or quiet reverence

☐ Enjoying the right music or worship style

☐ Some ritual step that shows devotion to Jesus

☐ Ability to pray or speak about Jesus impressively

**Sincerity**

☐ Really trying your best to serve God

☐ Reaching some emotional experience during worship

☐ Feeling personally close to God

☐ True enjoyment of prayer, Bible reading, worship, etc.

**Christian Heritage**

☐ Best denominational background or church circles

☐ Correct or rigorous theology

☐ Devotion to certain pastors, teachers, programs, or Christian artists

☐ Family or tribe's history of serving Christ

**Affiliations**

☐ Commitment to certain political or social causes

☐ Choosing healthy friendships and relationships

☐ Being in a good workplace, school, or neighborhood

**Markers of Success**

☐ Career, work, or school achievements

☐ Upstanding family

☐ Being liked or respected by others

☐ Accomplishments in sports or other activities

☐ Respectable manliness or womanliness

**STEP 2:** Although God's law is meant to help you love others, you might sometimes use it wrongly to put a burden on others.[2] So go back through the list, and this time consider people you love—your spouse, children, close friends, etc. Circle anything your heart counts on for their salvation, or anything you have turned into a burdensome requirement for them.

**STEP 3:** Finally, think of other believers. Underline any item in the list that you use to feel better than others, or any that make you feel inferior.

When the group is ready, share some of your responses. What false sources of righteousness tend to threaten your trust in Christ alone?

Imagine you more deeply believed that you are already counted righteous in Jesus. What might change about the way you treat others or yourself?

## WRAP-UP AND PRAYER *10 MINUTES*

Pray that you would know the freedom from having to perform for God that comes in the gospel, and that you would use God's law to love others rather than as a burden on them.

FOR NEXT TIME: The next lesson will skip ahead to Acts 16:6. There's a short section between this lesson's passage and one (Acts 15:36–16:5) that you may want to read on your own before the next time you meet.

*Lesson*

# 8

# SUFFERING AND FREEDOM

## BIG IDEA

God sends his people into dark places where we bring light and freedom. This mission comes with suffering, but Jesus is beside us.

## BIBLE CONVERSATION *20 MINUTES*

Acts 16 begins with Paul back in modern-day Turkey where he had preached before, this time accompanied by Silas, Timothy, and Luke the narrator. These missionaries will end up in new territory, crossing the Aegean Sea into Europe and reaching the city of Philippi. Philippi was a Roman colony, under Rome's direct governance and historically settled by the empire's military veterans. Roman rule could be harsh. Non-citizens might face severe punishment if they made trouble, and soldiers were under strict discipline. Those assigned to guard duty could be executed if prisoners escaped for any reason. Have someone read **Acts 16:6–40** aloud, or have a few readers take turns, and then discuss the questions below:

What do you notice about Philippi that shows the people there really do need help only Jesus can bring?

Which of the people in Philippi remind you of people you know in your city, and why? Consider their problems, their controlling desires, the pressures they face, etc.

It turns out Paul and Silas were Roman citizens who should not have been harshly treated. Why do you think they didn't mention their citizenship until after they were beaten and imprisoned?

****

Now read the article aloud, taking turns by paragraph. When you finish, discuss the questions that follow.

Lesson

**ARTICLE**

8

# THE CHURCH IN THE WILD

*5 MINUTES*

In Acts 16, God sends his church beyond familiar towns and people known to them, and into the wild. Philippi was on the fringe. For Jews, it was the outer edge of personality types and religious flavors. There, God would establish his people out of the most unlikely candidates: Gentiles, women, and slaves. This teaches us that God sends his church, you and me, to go and suffer and bring freedom to people trapped, bound in darkness and unseen and unaddressed by most of us. We are to be a church in the wild, and a church for the wild.

The Philippian slave girl was in both spiritual bondage and social bondage. When Paul cast out the evil spirit, he was freeing her from both demonic possession and from her owners who used her unjustly and cared only about the money they could make from a child. But there were also other, more subtle bondages happening in Philippi.

When we read that Paul and Silas got thrown into prison by a mob that only wanted to protect its patriotic community, we have to wonder about the other prisoners in the Philippian jail. Were they also simply nuisances to those trying to preserve the city's injustices? And the jailer was just as imprisoned as his prisoners. When he thought they had escaped, he was compelled to commit suicide. He was bound to the harsh Roman demands for performance, imprisoned to a life-and-death fear of failure.

This is where God sends his people—and where he gets his new people. We go to where sins and sorrows and thorns infest people's lives, as far and as deep as the curse is found. We go wherever demonic spirits thrive, wherever sin has taken dignity away, wherever injustice has stripped people of their sense of worth, and wherever performance has made us slaves of greed and success. Wherever people are separated from the redemption of God, that is how far and deep God will send his people. Notice three things about the journey.

**First, God sends his people to suffer.** As you are sent into places of bondage, you will be hurt and harassed. You will lose your comforts. You will be misunderstood and mistreated. Your ministry might seem to fail, or it will fail you. You will be made to look like you are the one bringing bondage, the way Paul and Silas, and not the demon girl, looked out of place in Philippi. Your children might get the backwash—poor schools, less worldly success—because God keeps sending you into broken places. It's wounding to be in the wild.

**Second, God sends his people to bring freedom.** In our suffering, God works. In Philippi, he caused an earthquake. Doors opened and shackles came off. The jailer who was about to kill himself for his job-performance failure got saved. The city leaders who hoped to hide their injustice had to personally escort Paul and Silas out, so that the people who had come to Jesus would feel free to worship. Verse 26 sums it up: "The foundations of the prison were shaken." God rattled that city free.

**Third, God gives his people Jesus.** When he opens the doors of all those prisons, we find peace for our souls in Christ. What must we do to gain it? "Believe in the Lord Jesus" (v. 31). At his name demons quake, cities shake, and hearts come awake. Whatever the world is struggling with, or whatever *you* are struggling with—whatever injustice or abuse, or whatever love you have for money or power or pleasure or success or competence—Jesus can break it.

Or, Jesus will break the power suffering has over you. You see, Paul and Silas worshipped Jesus while they were still in chains, *before* they knew they were going to be free. Whatever power suffering had—stealing joy and peace—was broken when Jesus came into their lives. They knew that we don't measure God's faithfulness by how much he spares us from suffering, but by his presence with us in our suffering. I am convinced Paul and Silas sang in prison not to show off, but for strength. And that strength came from praising together, reminding each other of Jesus, turning their hearts toward the presence and promises of God.

I used to watch *Man vs. Wild*, a reality television program where they drop a guy named Bear Grylls into some barren place and he shows us how to survive. I remember one time he didn't get any food and was freezing in his tent and couldn't make a fire. He said that to survive in times like that, he looks at a picture of his family. He said you should always come with a picture of something close to your heart to be the heat and energy you don't have.

As a church, we come together for worship and gather at the Lord's Table, and we meet in community groups, to get a picture of our freedom in Christ. And what picture do we look at? When we think about a world that will be freed as we go into it, and as we tell it about Jesus, and as we suffer while being out there, we look at the picture of the cross. We look at our Lord who took all those bondages on himself and suffered to set the captives of this world free. He gives his power, encouragement, and love to you and me—to be the church in the wild.

## DISCUSSION *10 MINUTES*

How do you feel about the idea that God sends you to hurting people in hard places? Explain.

What power does suffering have over you, and how have you seen it work in you?

Lesson

# 8 EXERCISE

# YOUR MISSIONARY JOURNEY

*20 MINUTES*

Studies of Paul's missionary journeys often include a map that shows where he travelled. Perhaps you've seen one. For this exercise, you will build on that idea to map out your own involvement in God's mission. Where and how do *you* get to tell people about Jesus, help them escape darkness, or support others who do this work? Or how have you done this in the past, or how might you in the future?

On your own, follow the prompts below to sketch out your map and add items to it. Pick several items to include. You might put them on a simple map of your neighborhood, your city, your nation, or the whole world. Or if physical locations aren't the best way to tell your missionary story, you can just list items and let that be your "map." When the group is ready, you'll share some of your responses and discuss them.

**God's barriers.** Are there places or types of work that God has let you know are *not* your way to serve his kingdom? Has God ever stopped you and sent you in a new direction? If so, place some of these barriers on your map.

**God's call.** Is there a place or type of work you believe *is* God's calling for you, or might be? Perhaps God has put a way to serve him in front of you—one that seems to beckon you. Maybe you've even heard someone say, "Come and help us here." If so, put it on your map.

**People.** What people might you go to? Or whom have you gone to already? Add some people, especially those who need the freedom found in Jesus because they are . . .

- Spiritually enslaved in some way
- Socially enslaved in some way
- Enslaved to performance or to the harsh expectations and demands of life, like the Philippian jailer
- Religious people like Lydia who know about God but still need to hear the good news of Jesus

**Suffering.** What suffering have you gone through because you were serving Jesus? Or what might you suffer if you followed the possibilities on your map? What cost is holding you back—or getting you excited about the glory of suffering for Jesus? Add that item.

**Earthquake.** What amazing things have you seen God do? Or what might you like to see God do somewhere on your map? These are "earthquakes" you can add.

**Song.** Finally, add a song for your journey. Write something wonderful about Jesus that makes you *want* to serve him or be on mission, or some praise that will keep you going when mission gets hard.

## My Missionary Journey

When the group is ready, explain some of what you drew and wrote. What does your journey look like so far? Where might God be taking you?

## WRAP-UP AND PRAYER *10 MINUTES*

Use the maps from the exercise as a prayer list, picking a few items to pray about for each other.

FOR NEXT TIME: The next lesson will skip ahead to Acts 17:16. If you want to read the brief section in between as part of your study of Acts, read Acts 17:1–15 on your own before the next time you meet.

*Lesson*

# 9

# THE KNOWN GOD

## BIG IDEA

In our search for God, human beings make up all kinds of religion. But there's good news: God has come to us as Jesus to find us, save us, and be known by us.

## BIBLE CONVERSATION *20 MINUTES*

In Acts 17, Paul finds himself in Athens, the intellectual hub of Greece. Athens housed the world's foremost schools of philosophy: the Epicureans who searched for life's meaning in private pleasures, and the Stoics who looked for it in public virtues and justice. The components of this wisdom were enshrined throughout the city. Athens was full of monuments and statues honoring many gods and goddesses, each with their own set of values, and was home to great temples where priests and servants kept the deities satisfied with food and sacrifices. Some of those temples are still among the world's most famous buildings.

In Athens, Paul will speak to the governing and religious council called the Areopagus, named for a rock outcropping above the city (Mars Hill in English) where the council often convened. If Paul spoke to the council at this location, he did so while standing just beneath the grandest of the city's temples. Have someone read the account of what happened there from **Acts 17:16–34**, or have a few readers take turns, and then discuss the questions below:

How are people where you live like the people of Athens, and how are they different?

Look at Paul's sermon. Which points would unbelievers you know react to most strongly, either positively or negatively, and why?

Of everything Paul preaches, what do you most need to hear? Explain.

****

Next, take turns by paragraph reading the article aloud. Then discuss the questions that follow it.

Lesson 9

ARTICLE

# A WORD TO THE WISE

*5 MINUTES*

When Paul stood before the council at the Areopagus, he declared to the most respected thinkers of the day that behind their wisdom, and all that people do or think, is the God of the Bible. He is the Creator and the divine prototype. We are not the originators of ourselves, nor are we original in anything we do. Our ethnicity, our wisdom, our technology, our science, and our arts all have their origin and perfection in the true God.

For the Athenians, even their ability to think religiously and then build made-up gods out of stone was only because God created all people with a preoccupation to seek him. This means there are some basic connections between humans. It means we have real bridges of communication with those who may not believe in God. We can appreciate the beauty in them, and we share the passion in them.

Yet when Paul speaks of feeling our way to God, the imagery is of someone groping in the dark. Human beings are blind about the Lord. In our fear and lostness, we use our God-given creativity to make gods out of what isn't God. We make up meanings for life. We create reasons to think we are happy. We make ourselves and others believe that in all our thinking and living and suffering and loving we might have found God in the darkness, but he cannot be found that way. He remains "the unknown god."

The Athenians were smart and spiritual people. They had come up with all sorts of explanations, monumented by their gods, to make them happy and to make sense of today and tomorrow. They even worshipped *nothingness*—the god they didn't know. Here is what's sad about that: if they have an unknown god, then they are unknown by their god. Their god has left them doing life by themselves. He is a deadbeat dad who has left them as spiritual orphans.

But Paul is saying God is more present and real than that. He is not a statue or a theory or an experience. He is not a bank account or a career or an acceptance into this or that club. And this means you are more than you can make of yourself. You are the offspring of a known God. You might be in the dark, but he is not. He will seek you. He will find you, to know you. As God who has come to us in the flesh, Jesus's life and death and resurrection rescues us from our ignorance.

The resurrection was hard for the Athenians, perhaps because it is a resurrection unto judgment. Could they handle a Mars Hill in the sky, where Jesus is judge of their philosophies and religion, and where he will condemn them and declare them unaccredited like they do to others? But Paul tells them there is a way to be right before God: repentance. Turn away from trying to figure it out on your own. Bow down to Jesus. Admit you are not as right as you thought you were. Let him find you and love you and lead you out of your darkness.

The Bible tells us that a number of these smart and resolved people came to Jesus. How could that happen? It's because Jesus is the wisdom that can't be outsmarted. In this world, people seek twenty thousand explanations and gods. But the Bible teaches that a single word, the word of the gospel, is sufficient to the wise.

Where that gospel word is preached and shared, in every condition and language and context of this world, the Holy Spirit comes on people's lives like a match to fuel—*kaboom!* That's the brilliance of the gospel. It's what the love of God in Christ does. The story of the life and death of Jesus, given to his people at a human level, means we carry around a divine wisdom. It is in our hearts and in our lives, and it should come out of our mouths to others.

So yes, we should engage the world. We should connect with others through technology and science and art and all that stuff. But when we tell people about Jesus, that is the one word that will outdo all others and will undo all the ways human wisdom hides from God. Tell how Jesus came. Tell how he lived and died for people like you and like them, people who do what you do and what they do. He lived and died and rose again to redeem you and them, to call you and them to live for his glory.

You need not wonder anymore whether God sees you and can reach you and will love you, whether he will touch you and make you beautiful to him. In Christ, he will. Jesus is the end of your ignorance. Jesus means you are known by the God of heaven. Respond to him, because he is worth it. Bow down, and live bowed down, and worship him with all you are and in all you do.

## DISCUSSION *10 MINUTES*

Think about people you know. How do they have a desire for God, even if they don't call it that?

If your appreciation for knowing God grew, how might your life change?

Lesson

9

EXERCISE

# FALSE GODS AND THE TRUE GOD

*20 MINUTES*

Paul's sermon in Athens addresses some of the ways many people search for spiritual meaning. He observes where this search will end up when you use your own ideas, and he shows how Jesus brings the life you've been seeking. Even if you already know Jesus, the good news Paul preaches can deepen your Christian joy.

On your own, compare Paul's description of the search for false gods with his proclamation of the true God. Read through each item in the chart below. Note ways you sometimes think like someone searching for false gods, and how you would be encouraged if you better grasped the wonder of the true God. If a particular item stands out to you, also look up and read the Bible verse that goes with it.

| Searching for False Gods | Knowing the True God |
|---|---|
| **I am my own creator.** I have the burden of figuring out who I am, and then remaking myself to live by that. | **God is my Creator.** I am also a new creation in Christ. I have the comfort of knowing that my whole being belongs to him. **Read Romans 14:8.** |
| **God demands my service.** I must meet his requirements if I want his blessings. | **God became a servant.** Jesus set aside his glory and died for me. He has met all of God's requirements on my behalf. **Read Mark 10:45.** |
| **We are divided.** Religion is about one group of people forcing its ideas on other groups. | **We are together.** We come from one God and one common ancestor. With all people I share one dignity, need one Savior, and am promised one Spirit in all who believe. **Read 1 John 4:14–15.** |
| **God should fit me.** To have a healthy spirituality, my human hands or my imagination must fashion the kind of god that works best for me. | **I am made to fit God.** Jesus is changing me into the person I long to be, one who experiences his glory and lives out his excellence. **Read 2 Peter 1:3.** |
| **God is distant.** He wants little to do with me and makes himself hard to approach. | **God has come near.** Jesus is human and sympathetic. The Holy Spirit is in me and comforting. And God's plan is to live with me forever. **Read Revelation 21:3.** |
| **There is no divine judgment.** Evil will always be with us, and there's only so much I can do about it. | **Righteous judgment is coming.** The purest, fairest, most love-defending Judge, who is also my Savior, is returning to make all wrongs right. **Read Psalm 98:7–9.** |
| **Death is the end.** I need to achieve as much enjoyment, love, and legacy as I can while my life lasts. | **Death is the beginning.** My soul will go to Jesus when I die, and my body will rise in glory when he returns. This eternal life will exceed any joy I can imagine. **Read 1 Corinthians 2:9.** |

Now also think about people you know, especially unbelievers. How are they searching for false gods, and how might they be encouraged to hear about the true God? Go back through the chart and note some of those items as well.

When the group is ready, share some of your responses. How does Paul's preaching about the true God encourage you? How might it encourage someone you know?

## WRAP-UP AND PRAYER *10 MINUTES*

As part of your prayer time together, you might include prayer for conversations with people searching for God.

FOR NEXT TIME: The next lesson will skip ahead to Acts 19. If you want to read the section in between as part of your study of Acts, read chapter 18 on your own before the next time you meet.

*Lesson*

# 10

# GOSPEL INSTIGATORS

## BIG IDEA

Gospel power will upend every part of our lives. When the Holy Spirit arrives, civic, religious, political, and economic uproar ensues.

## BIBLE CONVERSATION *20 MINUTES*

In this section of Acts, we have the story of Paul's stay in Ephesus and the fun/turmoil that ensued when the Holy Spirit was invited in. It's in Ephesus that Paul starts his third missionary journey. He had already visited Ephesus briefly and had promised to return for a longer period, "if God wills" (Acts 18:21). His two-year stay follows his usual pattern of teaching to the Jews first, then when he encountered opposition taking the gospel to the Gentiles.

Ephesus, an ancient Greek city and the Roman capital in Asia, was located in what is now Turkey. Directly on the Mediterranean Sea, it was the hub for trade all over Asia. It was also home to the grand temple of the Greek goddess Artemis (also called Diana by the Romans), which was considered one of the seven wonders of the world. The worship of Artemis was an important source of income to the city as many people spent money on articles associated with Artemis when they came to worship her.

It is into this city that Paul brings the life-changing, world-changing gospel message. Those changes are not welcomed by everyone as you will soon read. Have someone read **Acts 19:1–41** aloud, or have a few readers take turns. Then discuss the questions below:

What happened when John's disciples were baptized in the name of the Lord Jesus?

Contrast what the Holy Spirit did in this section vs. what Artemis could do. What is ironic about Demetrius's complaint about the Christians in verse 26?

Was it really religion that fueled the riot against the Christians, or something else?

Now take turns by paragraph reading the article aloud. Then discuss the questions that follow.

Lesson

10

ARTICLE

# HOW TO START A GOSPEL RIOT

*5 MINUTES*

If we honestly take stock of our world, we can all agree that change is needed. People have many different ideas about what should change and how that change should happen. But Christians know that change comes through the power of the Holy Spirit. When the Spirit shows up, old ways of doing things are turned on their heads. You might know that *should* be true, but in our world of issues and issue-based faith and religion, what *is* the church called to be and do that would righteously disrupt your city, country, and world?

Often it seems Christians are regarded more as a common nuisance and pest than a culture-transforming community of riot-raising love, beauty, and truth. How do we instigate that kind of riot? The passage today gives us a blueprint. We see that when the Holy Spirit showed up in Ephesus, God's people (1) confessed their own brokenness and (2) shared God's goodness in offering redemption without money or cost.

When the Holy Spirit came to Ephesus, repentance followed. New Christians confessed the wrongs they had done to themselves, others, and the true God. Those who practiced magic burned their expensive books—a public declaration that they had lived foolishly—as if there were no God (v. 19). They confessed personal and community Fail. Folly. Flunk.

The Ephesians were not burning anyone else's stuff. They caused and called for cultural transformation by leading with their own mess. We too will turn the world upside down for good and the glory of God when we stop making it our priority to confess and point out how wrong the world is, and instead confess that we have believed and lived as if the idols of this world—our money, houses, achievements, comforts, and pleasures—would make us happy.

## Repentance Compost

When believers count as trash what the world thinks is valuable (like the books and magic arts of Ephesus), their repentance creates compost that increases effectiveness of the word of the Lord (v. 20). But when you throw away what is valuable to the world around you, that irritates people. Even if you have said nothing directly about them, only about your own brokenness, it gets them thinking and weighing their lives and makes them ask, *What are we living for and how is it working out for us?* When people are at a loss, they will come at you. Especially if the way you are living will hurt their pocketbook.

So it was in Ephesus. Once the silversmiths realized that this paradigm shift would hurt their money—which is the real god here, not Artemis—they stirred up the whole city against the Christians (vv. 23–27).

## Sharing and Showing Gospel Power

There is more than repentance though. There is the good news of the gospel! In verses 11 and 12, we have a picture of how God has come to his people with power to redeem them. The symptoms of sin—sickness and evil spirits—are being healed, to show the world that God has the power to heal and take away all that is broken in the world and its people.

There is an intentional contrast here with the idols sold in Ephesus and the power of the Holy Spirit through the apostles. The items touched by the apostles like handkerchiefs and aprons were healing people, *unlike* the silver statues sold in Ephesus that were only benefitting their sellers. People who had evil spirits were being delivered from demonic possession, *unlike* the Sons of Sceva who tried to take the power for themselves as if it was a magic incantation to throw Jesus's name in there. These believers are living proof that what is happening to and through them is not idol magical practice—this is the real power of the true God at work among and in his people.

Ephesus was like a sexual amusement park. Like an amusement park, they were selling temporary and expensive thrills—rising, falling, being lifted, and caught and made to *feel* good. But the feeling only lasts as long as the ride—then you have to pay for more tickets for another ride. It's a never-ending, never-satisfying cycle.

Ephesus and its idol worship was offering not healing but masking; it offered a pain killer, but not a killer of what was causing the pain. The temple worship and money-making, get-rich schemes in Ephesus were not redeeming people. They were pretending to save, but it was not true salvation.

## Telling the World about Free Redemption

Those peddling religious wares admitted that their gods were man-made (v. 26). The people in Ephesus had to pay for their redemption (v. 24). They had to sacrifice and give money to the temple priests to have redemption. To be acceptable, they had to purchase their religion. Yet, even as they paid, they did not receive real redemption. Christianity declares that Jesus came, lived, died, and rose again to freely give redemption to all who believe. God paid for our redemption. He can't be bought. He can't be sold, and what he has is not for sale. He can and will only be gracious and merciful.

Do you want to cause a counter-cultural riot for good in this world? Talk about Jesus paying for redemption. Tell people that God, the true God, is not asking them and didn't ask you to do anything to receive redemption. That they, like you, did not and cannot buy or earn or be good enough to get religion or get God to love them. That you aren't good enough for God to love and he still keeps up his side of the relationship and lifts your side up too by grace. When you say this, people will go crazy wanting it or go crazy discrediting it. Because what else in this world is free or paid for by anyone else?

The silversmiths of Ephesus were concerned that Artemis would be "deposed from her magnificence" (v. 27). That's what the world expects from a god. But Jesus was debased, discredited, and became sin for us. He was the opposite of Artemis. He became not magnificent, but beneficent. He gave of himself so that you and I can come and be given grace and mercy by God for our brokenness and salvation from and in this broken world.

This is not what people are used to. It seems foolish, and it is. More foolish than making my god with my own hands is my God making me righteous by getting nails driven through his hands.

This love turned Ephesus upside down, and it still does wherever it is shared. It upsets people. It upsets cities, towns, and neighborhoods because it changes the value behind things. If salvation and the love of God has been paid for and freely given, if restored dignity and eternal life to human beings has been paid for and received by faith in Christ, then that changes the value and reason behind everything. If the most important thing is free, then all that is valued in our world is a trinket, a tool, and a mirage.

The church should make the market bottom drop out when it comes to what is expensive or enslaving to people's lives. We will pay less and call people to pay less for amusements, because their joy and peace and freedom is not of this world and not made by hands and is not afforded at their cost. Because in Christ we offer freedom to be who God has made us to be. Free because Jesus paid by living, dying, and rising again for humanity. The gospel—that's how you start a riot.

## DISCUSSION *10 MINUTES*

Describe a time when you heard a Christian confess their sins. How did that affect the people who heard? How did it affect you?

How did the gospel show up in Ephesus? How has the gospel showed up in your life and community?

*Lesson*

10

EXERCISE

# WHAT DO YOU WORSHIP?

*20 MINUTES*

All over the world people are still worshipping statues, occult practices, and parts of the natural world. In the developed world, those idols have been exchanged for idols of success, money, things, relationships, children, comfort, excitement, pleasure, and anything else you can think of. Without the Spirit of God at work in our lives, our hearts, as John Calvin famously said, are idol factories.

Different times, cultures, and people have different idols, but what they all have in common is that they promise us things that only God can give us. They are like the amusement-park life described in the article. Our idols take us up and down. We are distracted, amused, and momentarily satisfied but left empty. They can't answer the deepest questions of our lives or deliver us from death—for that we need Jesus. Only his full and free redemption can free us to live for him and make a lasting impact on the world around us.

The first step toward freedom is identifying what you are looking to for help, hope, love, and security that is not the living God. Fill out the table below for a few of those things you trust in for life that are not God. The first line is filled out with what the people of Ephesus might say. See if you can contrast what you get from your idols with what God freely gives. Below the table are a few Bible references to help you think about the redemption God gives.

| What Replaces the Living God | What I Hope It Offers | What I Really Get | What God Gives Instead |
|---|---|---|---|
| Silver statue of Artemis | Protection, prosperity | A silver statue that I paid for | Free redemption for sins, the price already paid |
| | | | |
| | | | |
| | | | |
| | | | |
| | | | |
| | | | |
| | | | |
| | | | |

**Bible Verses to Use:**
Romans 1:16–17
Romans 5:1–5
Romans 8
Philippians 4:11–13
Hebrews 13:5
1 Peter 1:3–4

**Exercise questions**

1. What did you learn about yourself from this exercise?
2. What did you learn about what you are really living for?
3. What did you learn about God?

## WRAP-UP AND PRAYER *10 MINUTES*

Pray in small groups together, asking God to send his Holy Spirit to your heart, your family, friends, neighbors, coworkers, city, and world.

FOR NEXT TIME: The next lesson will skip ahead to Acts 26. If you want to read the section in between as part of your study of Acts, read chapters 20 through 25 on your own before the next time you meet.

Lesson

# 11

# RENEGADE RELIGION

## BIG IDEA

The gospel—the good news of Jesus Christ—is the only thing worth being loyal to. It trumps all other loyalties.

## BIBLE CONVERSATION *20 MINUTES*

We pick up the action in Acts 26 after Paul has been arrested in Jerusalem (the story of his arrest and subsequent transfer to Roman custody is told in chapters 21–25). In a nutshell, Paul went to Jerusalem against the better judgment of the leaders in Asia. The Jews were plotting to kill him and so Paul, being a Roman citizen, appealed to the protection rights of Rome. The Roman authorities, at that time led by Felix, kept Paul from being assassinated by arresting him and putting him under house arrest. Paul kept climbing the court levels—going from local to federal and now possibly headed to the supreme court in Rome.

Here in chapter 26, Paul has made a stop in the court of the local governor, Festus. Festus invites King Agrippa, the local figurehead king over the Jerusalem area, to hear Paul's case. Paul explains to Festus and Agrippa the Christian faith. As he stands there in chains, he explains that to be a follower of Jesus your first loyalty must be to the Scriptures and the lordship of Jesus Christ. This idea makes Paul a renegade in the Roman Empire, where loyalty is owed first and foremost to Caesar. Yet Agrippa and Festus are fascinated by Paul.

There are two groups dealing with the movement of Christianity in their worlds—the Jews, who want Paul killed, and the Romans who want him managed away. When Paul defends the faith, he explains that he is only doing and being and talking according to what the Scriptures and God himself has told him to do. Have someone read **Acts 26:1–32** aloud, or have a few readers take turns. Then discuss the questions below:

What strategies does Paul use in this section to disarm King Agrippa and help him understand the gospel?

How did Festus respond to Paul's speech? How did Agrippa respond? What did Paul's reply say about who were the real prisoners in that throne room (v. 29)?

Have you ever been in a situation where you had to defend your faith? What did you say?

****

Now take turns by paragraph reading the article aloud. Then discuss the questions that follow.

Lesson

# 11

ARTICLE

# THE GOSPEL—PRIVATELY OWNED AND PUBLICLY OFFERED

*5 MINUTES*

If you grew up like I did in a section of the United States called the Bible Belt (because of all the churches on almost every corner), you might have thought, like I did, that Christianity was a safe, somewhat boring religious option. But when you read Acts, you see clearly that being a follower of Christ is not the "safe" option for your life or anyone else's. What makes it *the* anti-establishment religion? One way to describe it is that it's privately owned and publicly shared.

## The Gospel Is Privately Owned

Paul's speech to King Agrippa opens with his spiritual journey—the amazing story of how Paul went from persecuting Christians to becoming a follower of the Way of Jesus Christ and being persecuted himself. He wants to emphasize to Agrippa, that he heard God himself speaking to him and he must be loyal only to the God who met him on the road to Damascus. Paul wants Agrippa to know that this gospel was not Paul's idea—it comes straight from God. It's God's words, God's plan, and God's freely offered redemption.

Paul is declaring, as he stands in chains before Agrippa, that the gospel was not made up by people and it can't be changed by people. The words of the prophets came from the mind of God. The red-letter words Paul heard from Jesus on the road to Damascus were God speaking. It is privately owned by God himself and can't be massaged or changed to better fit Roman culture—or any culture.

## Loyal to the Gospel Message

The center of the gospel message that Paul shares is Jesus Christ. The gospel is loyal to Jesus of Nazareth. The two cannot be separated. Jesus is the fulfillment of the Jewish prophecies and hopes for a Savior. The resurrection proves that Jesus is the hoped-for Messiah and God himself (vv. 6–8; 22–23). Paul embeds the gospel message into his testimony, so those listening would have to contend with God's words—not Paul's words,

> "I have appeared to you for this purpose, to appoint you as a servant and witness to the things in which you have seen me and to those in which I will appear to you, delivering you from your people and from the Gentiles—to whom I am sending you to open their eyes, so that they may turn from darkness to light and from the power of Satan to God, that they may receive forgiveness of sins and a place among those who are sanctified by faith in me." (vv. 26:16–18)

Agrippa understood that Paul is saying in effect that *Jesus is Lord. You are a sinner, and you need him to pardon you. You need to bow down and seek him for salvation. He has been offered according to the Scriptures, to what the Bible says and teaches.*

This is the message that made Festus exclaim, "Paul, you are out of your mind; your great learning is driving you out of your mind" (v. 24). And then Agrippa, "In a short time would you persuade me to be a Christian?" (v. 28). It's an unsettling message and it's meant to disrupt and change people and the world. Because of Paul's clear presentation of the gospel, Agrippa rightly understood that following Christ would change everything about his life. Jesus could not simply be "added in" to Agrippa's world leaving him free to continue giving his ultimate loyalty to Rome and enjoying a lifestyle contrary to God's ways.

It's tempting to give up just a little bit of our loyalty to the gospel message when we share it to make it more palatable, more attainable. Does it always have to be about sin, repentance, and Jesus's death and resurrection? I see it in people's eyes when I say, "The Bible says . . . or Jesus says . . ." But the truth is, that is the gospel message. We can't change it to make it easier to follow. Jesus doesn't follow you; you follow Jesus.

## The Gospel Is Publicly Shared

The gospel of the life, death, and resurrection of Jesus Christ will never be mainstream. It may ride on the same tracks for a while with the culture, but it will diverge and exit at some point. The message that we are saved by grace alone, through faith alone, in Christ alone, as revealed by Scripture alone, to the glory of God alone, will always cause the crowds who come for personal satisfaction, an easy life, and money in the bank to drift away.

But even so, Christians are called to be mainstream—God needs his people to be everywhere in the public square because this privately-held-by-God gospel is meant to be shared all over the world. Paul shows us the way forward by putting the gospel out there in the open before rulers, kings, and common people. He tells Jews the gospel message. He tells Gentiles the gospel message. He is not afraid to ask people to own that God, in his Word, says they are wrong. He is not ashamed to call them to repentance and to let Jesus and his Word run their lives. He knows they are too broken to run their own lives for themselves, and that calling them to repentance will point this out to them, but he says it anyway.

You might have already noticed that the gospel message can get an intense reaction. It gets a critical reaction because it is shared as if the world is in a critical condition. It treats the human condition as it really is—on the edge of eternal life or death. Paul's loyalty to Christ has so mastered him that his deepest concern in this courtroom is not about getting out earlier. Instead, he wants everyone listening to be like him—free from the slavery of sin and brokenness.

What about you? How goes it with your public sharing of the gospel message? God calls all believers to live not privately, but in the main-stream, doing the same jobs, hanging out in some of the same places, and raising their kids around people who don't know Jesus. God needs his people everywhere—in every workplace, neighborhood, strata of society, facing every hardship by faith so the watching world will know that Jesus is alive and heaven is our real home.

It's easy to critique how others share the gospel message—the athletes who kneel or point to heaven, the friend who might share awkwardly. But they are doing what we are all called to do—share our faith publicly. We must be loyal to the free gift of eternal life—the gift of our darkness turning into light and the defeat of Satan's power to enslave and send us to death (v. 18).

You see, the chains that Paul wore were not the chains of a slave to the world, but of one privately owned and bought by Jesus. Paul is bound to Jesus to be a light and live out the truth of the gospel. He had been found by the God he always longed to know. His life is no longer his own, it belongs to Jesus who called him to go to the world so they too may come and find salvation through what Christ has done and given.

## DISCUSSION *10 MINUTES*

The article talks about how because the gospel is owned by God, which means we can't change it to sound better to the hearers. Have you noticed that this is hard for you? What about the gospel seems to offend the people you know?

How goes it with your public sharing of the gospel? Can you remember the last time you shared your faith with someone who doesn't know Jesus? How did that go?

Lesson

**11**

**EXERCISE**

# SHARING YOUR TESTIMONY

*20 MINUTES*

Everyone likes a good story, and our world is full of them. We tell stories to each other about our day, lives, families, and how we grew up. But what makes a story about your life different from a testimony? A story about your life is centered on you—you are the main character. But your testimony is God's story in you. Christians have a testimony to share when they have come to Jesus for forgiveness and trusted him for salvation. In that moment (or time), the main character of your story becomes God. Your life no longer revolves around you (although it can certainly feel like it does); instead it revolves around Jesus who called you out of darkness into light and loosed the chains of sin and death.

This is the third time in Acts that Paul has shared his testimony. The basic parts are the same, but notice also that he is aware of his audience and what he needs to say to help them understand and relate to his story of how God changed him.

There are three basic elements:

1. What Paul was like before he met Jesus (vv. 1–11)
2. How Jesus met Paul (vv. 12–18)
3. How life has changed since he met him (v. 29)

In this exercise, you will follow the pattern Paul has laid out here and write your testimony. In Romans 10:9, Paul links telling our salvation story with our salvation when he says, "If you confess with your mouth that Jesus is Lord and believe in your heart that God raised him from the dead, you will be saved." So sharing your testimony is an integral part of your life with Jesus. Once you write out your testimony, pray and ask God for an opportunity to share it with someone who doesn't yet know Jesus. As you pray, remember the goal isn't simply to be sure you told someone else about Jesus. It's to love that other person and get to know them well enough, so that when they are open to hearing more about Jesus you are ready to share your testimony clearly. You don't need to force your story on someone who isn't ready to hear it yet. Be patient. Ask the Holy Spirit to let you know when they are ready to hear more and then trust him to work.

Pitfalls to avoid in sharing your testimony:

- **Spending most of your time on what you were like before you met Jesus.** This often happens if you have lived a more wild or colorful life. Your "war stories" will catch people's attention, but if you spend too much time on them, they will be all that people remember. Ask the Spirit to help you frame them in a way that let's others know how much you needed Jesus.
- **Thinking that you don't really have a testimony if you can't remember a specific time when you turned to Jesus in faith.** For those who grew up in a Christian family and never went to the wild side of life (thank God, by the way!), it can be easy to think you don't really have a testimony. But you have an

amazing testimony of knowing God's love and trusting Jesus from the earliest age. Think about sharing some of the faith markers in your life that showed Jesus's love and care for you and the sins you need to repent from.

- **Ending your testimony too soon.** Often when we share our testimonies with others, we end with the moment we accepted Christ. But really we should have a testimony that stretches through our life. What has following Jesus meant to you this year? This month? How has being a Christian changed the direction of your life?
- **Making your life sound "all better" now that you know Jesus.** Honestly those we talk to will be more interested in hearing how Jesus sustains us through the difficulties, sorrows, and trials of life. Be careful to not sound as if knowing Jesus solves our problems. Remember, you are still a sinner, even if your sins have now been paid for by Christ. We still struggle, we still sin, we still need to repent and receive by faith the promises of the gospel. Knowing Jesus brings us into a new kingdom where we have a new life now and eternal life forever, but we are still living in a hard and sad world. Living by faith means Jesus is always with us, watching, keeping, holding, and guiding.

To write your testimony answer these three questions:

1. What were you like before you met Jesus? What were you doing? What were your struggles? (Write just a few bullet points.)

2. How did Jesus meet you? Tell the story of how you got to know Jesus. Was it a Bible verse you heard? A friend who shared their faith? Something you read or saw? What does repenting for your sins look and sound like for you? (Write just a few bullet points.)

3. How do you live life with Jesus now? What does it mean to you today that Jesus is alive and with you? How could you describe that to someone in a way they could understand? (Write just a few bullet points.)

Now share your testimony with the whole group or divide into pairs and share with one person.

## WRAP-UP AND PRAYER *10 MINUTES*

Pray that God would give you a chance to share your testimony with at least one person in the coming week.

FOR NEXT TIME: The next lesson will pick up at Acts 27:13. If you want to read the section in between as part of your study of Acts, read verses 1–12 on your own before the next time you meet.

*Lesson*

# 12

# TRAGEDY ENDS IN GLORY

## BIG IDEA

God ordains the hardships the church faces, sustaining us through them for a glorious ministry and to a glorious end.

## BIBLE CONVERSATION *20 MINUTES*

In the last lesson we followed Paul's journey through the court system as he defended the gospel before one official after another. In the end, no one could really find anything wrong with Paul or his faith, but since he had appealed to Rome—to Rome he must go. Paul boards a ship on the way to Rome from Judea. To journey to Rome, they had to cross the Mediterranean Sea which was known for storms at that time of the year. Paul advises the centurion in charge not to sail, but the centurion takes the advice of the captain and owner of the ship and sets sail for Rome.

Soon the ship was caught in a powerful storm called a northeaster, which was notorious for pushing ships up into the rocks of the islands they were sailing near. We pick up the story right at the point where Paul and everyone else on the ship are facing death as the storm rages around them. There is an amazing rescue, and then Paul finally reaches

Rome. Acts ends with Paul doing what he has done since he became a follower of the Way—preaching to Jews and then Gentiles. Read **Acts 27:13–44; 28:16–17, 22–31** and then discuss the questions below:

What word from the Lord did Paul receive while in the middle of the storm?

You might think Paul would have just sat back and relaxed after he heard from God. But what did he say and do instead? Has knowing that God will keep you safe ever given you fresh courage to say and do difficult things?

This is the last we read about Paul's life in the Bible. How would you assess his legacy? And how does that differ from what the people around him might have thought?

*Lesson*

# 12

ARTICLE

# GOD IS IN THE STORM

*20 MINUTES*

You may never have been through a storm like Paul and his fellow travelers. But you, like every Christian, have experienced the storms of life, been shipwrecked, and landed in strange, challenging, personally devastating, and tragic places.

Yet we see in Acts 27 that God is in Paul's storm, and he is in yours as well. Your tempest—the storm, struggle, challenge, shakeup you are facing—is the hand of God in your life. In your storm, like Paul's, God will bring grace to you and this world through Jesus Christ.

## God Is in Control of the Storm

Notice that when the storm hits, everybody has a plan to handle it. The sailors first get rid of the cargo (v. 18). As the storm continues, they throw the ship's tackle over the side (v. 19), and finally they try to leave on a lifeboat (v. 30). But none of their plans calm the storm.

But then God appears. Paul got a message from God: all who sailed with Paul would live through the storm. The storm is still raging; but despite that, it's not in control. God is in control. God's plan to bring Paul to Rome and to spread the gospel was driving the ship—not the wind and the waves, but the Lord himself.

God, in his good providence, takes circumstances and bends them like he does the storm. The Lord will bring crisis and upend our plans, our ways, and the world's ways to cause our lives to reflect his plan for our good and his glory. God is in the northeaster. God is in your storm too, and he is in control. He is blowing against the wind of our plans with his will and causing a whirlwind—a tornado of good providence.

What we may call disaster and tragedy, God calls his perfect and permissive will. And what we give cause and pause to, God has orchestrated in such a way that he is the author of all things good and glorious, and yet not the author of sin. That's how the gospel spreads and deepens within his people.

## Not a One Was Lost

All of Acts teaches us that Christianity did not flourish out of the great personal, financial, political, and social gain of Jesus's followers. It grew out of great expense and loss. The gospel still grows this way. That was what everyone on the boat experienced in the northeaster. Read verse 20 again and see if it also maps onto your experience:

> When neither sun nor stars appeared for many days, and no small tempest lay on us, all hope of our being saved was at last abandoned.

All their plans to save themselves had come to nothing. They had to rid themselves of all they relied on. They gave everything they valued, and their very lives to the power and mercy of the storm. But then—a word from the Lord: you will be saved. As they gave up their power, competencies, control, escape routes, and comforts, they saw the power of God to save them. Not a one was lost. So it still is today. The storms of life will press us to give up everything but our faith in Jesus whose plans are good, whose gospel is true, and who will not lose any that the Father has given him.

We can even, in hindsight, thank the Lord for the storm, for the end of ourselves, for our dark nights and days where we were left with nothing. We can thank God because it comes with glorious results.

## Tragedy Then Glory

What are those glorious results?

We read in Acts 28 that Paul ends up in Rome preaching to the Jews. Some became followers of Jesus, but most were offended and so once again he turns to the Gentiles. Our last glimpse of Paul is under house arrest. Many scholars believe he died in Rome without getting justice before Caesar. No Spain, no French Riviera, no Apostle Paul School of Messianic Judaism, no Apostle Paul Ministry. How is this gospel success?

But the glorious result of Paul's imprisonment is that he could defend his faith to all his visitors, write letters to churches, and train young preachers all under the protection and security of the Roman government. Paul was more effective in chains, under house arrest, than he ever would have been running for his life through Spain.

It was ironic that Paul, under house arrest, was free to say and write what God wanted him to without the Jews or the government shutting him down. Dare I say it? Paul was freed by God to be what God wanted him to be and do even as it seemed he was trapped and caught in a tragedy. Paul was not safe and free in this world, but he was safe and free in the lifegiving hands of God. In this world, there is no freedom, no safety, no sense of worth that cannot be lost. True freedom comes by being captured and held captive by the love and care of Jesus Christ.

After the death of Chuck Colson, who served time for his part in the Watergate scandal and who also founded Prison Fellowship—a ministry to prison inmates—journalist Michael Gerson wrote this: "It is the central paradox of Christianity that fulfillment starts in emptiness, that streams emerge in the desert, that freedom can be found in a prison cell."[3]

## Jesus—The Tragic Hero Who Overcomes Our Fatal Flaw

Paul's life trajectory, as that of every Christian, imitates that of his Savior, Jesus, a life that looks tragic, but ends in glory. Aristotle defines a tragic hero in his book *Ars Poetica* (The Art of Poetry) as a good person with a "tragic flaw." In the story, something terrible happens to him—often his own death. But it is in experiencing this catastrophe that he overcomes the tragic flaw.[4]

The gospel spreads in us and through us to the world when we embrace Jesus Christ, whose tragic flaw is not his but ours. He took on the flaw of our sin. The catastrophe was his crucifixion and death. But when he rose from the grave, he overcame the tragedy of our sin and the world broken by sin. His story intersects with our lives and becomes our story. We too experience tragedy, but the results are always glorious.

Christianity could be described as "The World's Most Amazing Tragedy." A tragedy played out on the world's stage, with a growing cast but also with a growing group of critics. But unlike a tragedy, this one ends in glory. The gospel and Jesus's church continue to travel, to show up, to spread, to change lives. But the basic script stays the same as the one in the closing chapters of Acts. It is the blueprint of world redemption, and it happens by God's good providence, at great expense to God's people, and with glorious results of eternal life for all who believe.

## DISCUSSION *10 MINUTES*

List some of the plans you have made to handle the storms of your life. What was good about the plans (think about Paul who made plans in Acts 27 to keep everyone alive through the shipwreck)? What was not so good about your plans?

Can you look back on any of the storms of your life and see a "glorious result"? Write down one example.

*Lesson*

12

EXERCISE

# GLORY MOMENTS IN ACTS

*20 MINUTES*

Pick one passage that today maps on to your life (see the short explanation of the tragedy) and then describe the specific tragedy in Acts and then describe the glory it led to.

**1. Lame Man Healed (3:1–10)** – for when you feel broken by suffering

*Tragedy*

*Glory*

**2. Stephen Martyred (7:51–60)** – for when you are attacked for following Jesus

*Tragedy*

*Glory*

**3. Saul's Conversion (9:1–31)** – for when you or someone you love is running away from Jesus

*Tragedy*

*Glory*

**4. The Gospel for All (10:1–11:18)** – for when you feel excluded

*Tragedy*

*Glory*

**5. Church Conflict (15:1–32)** – for when the church hurts you

*Tragedy*

*Glory*

**6. Paul and Silas in Prison (16:6–40)** – for when your faith has landed you in hot water

*Tragedy*

*Glory*

## WRAP-UP AND PRAYER *10 MINUTES*

Prayer instructions:

The article says, "*We can even, in hindsight, thank the Lord for the storm, for the end of ourselves, for our dark nights and days where we were left with nothing. We can thank God because it comes with glorious results.*" Can you in hindsight see any glory moments in your life? In prayer thank God for what he has done and ask him for what you need today.

# LEADER'S NOTES

These notes provide some thoughts and background information that relate to the study's discussion questions, especially the Bible conversation sections. The discussion leader should read these notes before the study begins. Sometimes, the leader may want to refer the group to a point found here.

However, it is important that you not treat these notes as a way to look up the "right answer." The most helpful and memorable answers usually will be those the group discovers on its own through reading and thinking about the Bible text. You will lose the value of taking time to look thoughtfully at the text if you are too quick to turn to these notes.

## LESSON 1: LIFE AFTER JESUS HAS LEFT

Participants may want to know more about the sweeping story and themes leading up to Acts. Don't get so bogged down in background that you rush through Acts itself. But for more on how Jesus saw the events of his life and of Acts as biblical fulfillment, see Luke 24:44–53. For the glory of the kingdom under David and Solomon, see 2 Samuel 8 and 1 Kings 9:10–10:29. For how Jesus is David's Son who reigns forever, see Luke 1:30–33. For how Israel's witness will reach to the end of the earth, see Isaiah 43:1–21. For Jesus's return on the day of the Lord to judge sinners but save believers, see 1 Thessalonians 5:1–11. Joel's prophesy comes from Joel 2:28–32. As with Luke's gospel, Acts is addressed to Theophilus, which means "Lover of God." This may be a sponsor or student of Luke, or it may be Luke's way of addressing any reader.

Although Acts does not say what Jesus taught about the kingdom during the forty days after his resurrection, there's much to learn about it from what happens in these opening chapters. Jesus's kingdom is worldwide. He reigns with a spiritual presence on earth rather than a physical one, but still with strong evidence that he is indeed the risen King enthroned on the clouds and in heaven. He is not disinterested during his physical absence, but guides his kingdom's advance and is preparing to return in triumph. And despite his absence, the kingdom remains all about God's presence with his people. Each person in the kingdom matters and receives the Spirit's indwelling and equipping. The kingdom is powered by God, so that its advance requires patiently waiting on God at times. A key feature of the kingdom is the salvation of all who call on the Lord, anywhere in the world, from the day Peter announced the Spirit's arrival until the day King Jesus returns to renew the earth.

For the Jews who heard Peter preach from Joel, the message of ordinary people empowered to reach the whole world would have been an unexpected answer to the question the disciples asked Jesus in Acts 1:6, "Will you at this time restore the kingdom to Israel?" The answer is yes, but not how they expected. The kingdom is both bigger (worldwide, inclusive of all, conquering all evil) than they might have imagined, and at the same time appearing less impressive (largely invisible for now, led by former fishermen), and it won't arrive in fullness until Jesus returns. The regions listed in 2:8–11 extend in all directions from Jerusalem.

Notice that alongside this salvation and equipping of diverse believers, the passage also retains an emphasis on the twelve apostles and their authority. In the Bible, prophesy does not always denote telling the future or authoritative preaching. It can be any speech aroused by the Spirit that tells about God.

The fire-like appearance of the tongues likely connects to multiple themes in Scripture. It might show the presence of God in the Spirit-filled age or his purifying power in his people and the world. John's water baptism signified a preparatory cleansing from sin, but with the new age inaugurated, those baptized with the Spirit also live with holy fire. Jesus burns up sin in them as he reclaims the earth for his kingdom. In Luke's gospel, Jesus's arrival means the time of fiery, purifying judgment is approaching (Luke 3:15–17; see also 2 Peter 3:10–13).

## LESSON 2: GOD'S GIFT, THE CHURCH

Peter's sermon gives an excellent summary of Jesus's work as the Christ up to the present day. He mentions Jesus's miracles, death, resurrection, ascension, and reign at God's right hand. Peter focuses on the latter parts of this—Christ's *exaltation*—quoting Psalm 16 on the resurrection and Psalm 110 on the ascension and heavenly reign. And Peter highlights the exciting implications of Jesus's reign: repentance and forgiveness and spiritual power are for all who believe! God's long-planned mission to spread his gospel promises is underway, sure to reach distant lands and generations.

If your group tends not to celebrate some of these elements much, you might discuss why Peter finds them compelling. Jesus's ascension directs our attention to the treasures of heaven, where he is and we will follow. There we have a King who pleads for us, bestows gifts, defends us from evil, subdues our enemies, and prepares for us a home with him. Coupled with the joys of forgiveness and spiritual renewal, we have much reason for our whole lives to orbit around Jesus and our fellow believers who share this hope.

Be careful not to let the descriptions of the Jerusalem church lead to a group time in which participants merely gossip about how their churches have failed. Some participants may have hurts that are helpful to share and acknowledge, and it's good for your group to be a safe place to express frustrations. But keep in mind the main point of the passages that describe the church: they don't scold your church or give you a checklist to feel guilty about, but rather show the power of the Holy Spirit. Through the word of God, by which the whole world was created, the Spirit is reviving sin-trapped people and remaking them into a glorious community that will end in the heavenly life.

## LESSON 3: ALL THAT JESUS GIVES

Peter and John's interaction with the lame man is personal and purposeful. The man does not just get a healing the way he might get a silver coin. Instead, the disciples make sure he realizes that God is looking at him, in all of his brokenness and shame, and seeing him for the person he will be when Jesus's work is finished. They not only act in Jesus's name, but in Jesus's manner.

The man seems to realize the spiritual implications of his healing. He goes into the temple, not home to friends or family, and there he praises God. He also attaches himself to the church community, not only clinging to Peter and John initially but still standing beside them the next day after their arrest (4:14).

The healed man's life story is one of huge change and fullness, not just a little improvement. Peter's preaching mirrors this. He proclaims Jesus as the fulfillment of everything promised to God's people and all that the prophets foretold. This includes not just the eternal forgiveness Peter mentions in 3:19, but extends to "restoring all the things" (v. 21): spiritual renewal, personal holiness, victory over evil, life in God's presence, release from the world's curse, and more.

## LESSON 4: THE MISSION AND MESSAGE OF LIFE

Acts 5 points out some of the temple leaders' motivations: they are jealous (v. 17), afraid of the people (v. 26), and filled with violent rage (v. 33). They live in fear of being pushed out of power or found out as religious frauds. The apostles have shown them their guilt, and they are unwilling to stand among the believers and before God to admit their sin and embrace the forgiveness of Jesus. Only Christ's forgiveness relieves pride and jealousy, letting us stop living violently and fearfully about this life, no longer afraid of not having enough or not being enough in the eyes of others.

The temple leaders are so concerned about their own power, controlling their peace with Rome, and avoiding repentance that they resist any messianic talk. They don't *want* to hear the good news that God is taking control and is spreading real peace and repentance to the world. Beneath their jealousy and fear lies the deeper sin of unbelief—they have rejected Jesus as Savior and King. Although they take Gamaliel's advice, they seem to do so grudgingly. Gamaliel is already right about their hearts: they are opposed to the work of God.

The apostles are different not because of what they've achieved but because of what they've been given. The wording in verses 31 and 32 reminds us that God *gives* repentance, forgiveness of sins, and the Holy Spirit. With these gifts, the apostles toss self-concern aside. They have boldness and joy even in the face of beatings and worldly dishonor. They are not just knowledgeable about the gospel, but are lit up with the Spirit's fire to tell it. They are witnesses (literally, *martyrs*) to all that God is doing (v. 32), ready to give their bodies and their lives for the truth they proclaim.

When Stephen refers to Jesus as the Son of Man, it's likely the temple leaders recognize it as referring to the messianic figure in Daniel 7:13–14 who comes on the clouds of heaven and is given dominion, glory, and a worldwide kingdom. Jesus often called himself the Son of Man, and had used the imagery from Daniel 7 when the same council put him on trial—getting a similar reaction to the one Stephen gets (see Matthew 26:63–68). Stephen not only believes in Jesus but is spiritually connected to him. As a faithful believer, Stephen is in Christ and blessed "with every spiritual blessing in the heavenly places" (Ephesians 1:3). He is following his Savior into the glory of the resurrection life, and is already becoming like Jesus. Stephen's death mirrors the death of Jesus as he is unfairly tried, speaks of the glory of the Son of Man, prays for his killers, and calls for God to receive his spirit (see Luke 22:66–69; 23:34, 46).

## LESSON 5: LIGHT AND LIFE

Although Saul was zealous for Jewish traditions that looked godly to those around him, he didn't truly know God before meeting Jesus on the road to Damascus. True knowledge of God makes us humble and teachable, but Saul's knowledge had made him headstrong and violent. According to his own accounts in Acts 22, Galatians 1, and Philippians 3, he was destructive and was putting his faith in his own religious accomplishments rather than in God and Christ's work on the cross.

Saul's new life is marked by repentance and faith. He begins by sorrowfully seeking God—fasting and praying and being baptized. Not surprisingly, such a fundamental change and new allegiance to Jesus comes with some stress: old allies try to kill him, while his new allies don't trust him at first. But Jesus opens the eyes of Ananias and the apostles as well, and proves to be Saul's best ally.

Jesus has more dialogue than anyone else in Acts 9. As the key player in this account and one with a glorious plan, he is powerful, sovereign, insistent, and a staunch defender of his people. But he is also understanding, forbearing, quick to help, and full of unexpected mercy. He is still the amazing person we first met in the Gospels, even as he now does his world-changing and people-transforming work from heaven.

## LESSON 6: CROSSING BOUNDARIES

The divide between Jews and Gentiles was a longstanding and important one. In Acts 10, God takes special actions to communicate that he is ending it. He uses an angelic announcement, a grand vision that twice repeats his point, and a clear-to-see outpouring of the Holy Spirit that echoes the landmark event in chapter 2. If your group discusses angels, visions, or signs of the Spirit, keep the point of this passage in mind: God was guiding his people through a pivotal moment in their history.

To their credit, both Cornelius and Peter let the Lord lead. Both men, one as a Roman commander and the other as the lead apostle, have much authority within their circles. But both understand that the greatest honor is to be a servant of God. Cornelius bows. Peter stands beside him as a brother. Both men give testimonies of the Lord's work in them. They extend and accept hospitality. And by ordering the Gentiles' baptism, Peter affirms the Lord's authority to choose whom to welcome into his church.

It is not surprising that some believers would scold Peter for entering Cornelius's house and then staying with him. The Jewish traditions were based on the biblical principles of maintaining separateness and ritual cleanliness, and there was also biblical precedent for a man of God on mission to refuse hospitality from outsiders who might lead him astray (see 1 Kings 13:1–24). It might have looked as if Peter was being corrupted. But like Peter, the leadership in Jerusalem valued God's guidance above their own sense of what was good, and praised God for the event at Cornelius's house. (Note, though, that the circumcision party's views, which added the requirement of being Jewish to the gospel, did not completely go away. See Acts 15:1–35; Galatians 2:11–14; Titus 1:10–11). However, God made it very clear that nothing other than faith in Christ was required to be saved from our sins and welcomed into his family (see Philippians 2:1–11).

## LESSON 7: DEFENDING THE GOSPEL

Paul and Barnabas are concerned that the church keeps preaching the pure gospel—one that removes burdens rather than adding them (15:10, 19). As a former Pharisee, Paul knew the burden that comes with trying to be righteous enough to earn acceptance from God. He had left that false gain behind when he found Christ and received Jesus's record of righteousness purely by faith (see Philippians 3:2–9). He insists on preaching this without compromise.

The other former Pharisees among the believers likely have heard this gospel too, but seem to have a hard time letting go of the sense they must *do something* to merit God's approval. They might still be struggling with pride that comes from being recognized as the "better" believers who show others the right way. In Galatians, Paul strongly condemns their motives, saying they are tempted to show off what they have done, avoid persecution, and boast about what they've gotten others to do (see Galatians 6:12–13).

In this dispute, the gospel wins out. There's much to admire about how the apostles and elders resolve the matter: They are concerned to let God lead them rather than push for their own ways. They listen to the gospel of grace spoken by Peter. They check in Scripture to confirm that what God seems to be doing is what the Bible said he would do (the quotation is from Amos 9:11–12). They remain humble, aware of their own failures and need for Jesus. They have genuine joy over the conversion of people different from themselves rather than being protective of their Jewishness. And when they find that some believers might have been troubled by bad teaching, they act as good shepherds to care for those believers and relieve their burdens.

The letter sent to the Gentile believers is not a compromise but a message of pastoral care. The four rules from James are all connected to pagan religions. They are activities Gentile believers would struggle with that might pull them away from Jesus and closer to people who would hurt their faith. Those practices also might have been especially upsetting to the Jewish-heritage believers in the Gentile churches, so that refraining was a good way for the Gentile and Jewish believers to draw closer to each other instead. In any case, James is letting the Gentile believers know they no longer need to find fellowship in idol-worshipping homes and temples. They can find it at the table of the Lord, with Jew and Gentile believers together. This loving concern for the Gentile believers encourages them. They see that James claims them as fellow Christians, brothers and sisters and children under his care.

## LESSON 8: SUFFERING AND FREEDOM

There's evidence in Acts 16 that Philippi is a dark and unforgiving place: the abusive use of the slave girl, the violence toward Paul and Silas when they help her, and the fear shown by both the jailer and the magistrates. But in that city, God uses suffering—and his people's reaction to it—to change hearts.

Paul and Silas do not seek to be mistreated, but they are willing to suffer as part of their mission and they seem to realize that this might move the gospel forward. This is Paul's understanding when he writes to the Philippians during a later imprisonment: "What has happened to me has really served to advance the gospel" (Philippians 1:12). The prayer and singing Paul and Silas do in prison recall the apostles who responded to similar injustice by "rejoicing that they were counted worthy to suffer dishonor for the name" (Acts 5:41). It is also part of their witness about Jesus, and it may be why none of the prisoners escaped when they had the chance. Paul's insistence on an apology afterward may be a way to protect the new group of believers. It means the magistrates have acknowledged that Christians are not a danger to the city.

## LESSON 9: THE KNOWN GOD

Those who live in Western cultures may find that the approaches to religion and philosophy in Athens are familiar. There is not just a marketplace in Athens, but a "marketplace of ideas" where a mix of religious and worldview options are accepted, combined, debated, and sometimes scorned. Paul rightly sees that for all its deep thinking, this self-made religion ends in uncertainty and death without the Wisdom of God, Jesus Christ.

Paul's sermon is much more than an example of how to connect to listeners using their cultural context; it is an excellent critique of false religions like those we still encounter today. It exposes the emptiness of building our lives around created things that need constant feeding. It reveals the burden of a religion that tries to appease and impress God. And it unmasks the hollowness of trusting human reason, education, or popular theories of society. Amid all of these, only Jesus rises from the dead with real hope for those who grope in darkness.

## LESSON 10: GOSPEL INSTIGATORS

Acts contains both *descriptive* and *prescriptive* elements. Descriptive elements tell us about how historical events happened at one point and time in church history, whereas prescriptive elements tell us what should happen as a normal practice in the church going forward.

Prescriptive passages present principles and practices God intends for all believers in all times to follow. Acts 19:1–7 is a good example of prescriptive language. While some Christians have used the opening story in this chapter to argue that Christians need "the second blessing" of the Holy Spirit, this is not what this story is about. Instead, it's about John's disciples becoming Jesus's disciples. They were not yet followers of Jesus and had never heard that Jesus gives the Holy Spirit to all who call on him in repentance and faith. It was placing their trust in Jesus that saved them and filled them with his Spirit.

Verses 11–12 regarding handkerchiefs and aprons touched by Paul being used to drive out demons is a good example of a descriptive element. God was doing a unique, powerful work through Paul in the specific context of Ephesus to prove his power over the supposed spiritual authorities of the city, including the demons. While God always retains that power, and still overcomes spiritual forces that oppose him, nowhere in the rest of the New Testament do we see that power being assigned to objects like handkerchiefs and aprons, nor are we told to expect him to work this way in the future. Spiritual warfare is real and continues today, but assigning God's power to created objects (like handkerchiefs and aprons) does not.

When the Spirit arrives, the world is upended. The city of Ephesus is no exception—it's in an uproar. New Christians, filled with the Spirit of Jesus, radically changed their way of living—even giving up the magic books that were their tools of the trade. The change in them threatened the economy of the city and led to the riot against them.

Don't skip the discussion of what we put first in our lives and hearts—what are our idols. It's easy to point to those who have actual statues in their homes as idol worshippers. But just like Demetrius, who was worshipping money, we are all worshipping something besides the living God.

## LESSON 11: RENEGADE RELIGION

Paul's testimony before Agrippa is worth studying in detail because of how he shares his faith. He understands the person he is sharing with (notice how he reminds Agrippa of all he already knows about the Jewish religion), and he understands what points to make that will catch and keep Agrippa's attention.

Paul's quoting of Jesus's words to him on the road to Damascus is more fleshed out from the account in Acts 9. Paul adds the detail of

Jesus saying "it is hard for you to kick against the goads" (26:14). A goad was a sharp object meant to keep cattle in line but was used also as a proverb to describe useless resistance to a higher power. Paul's emphasis in what he shares about his conversion is on his commissioning by God through the Lord Jesus Christ to go and share the gospel with the Gentiles. Paul is before the powers of Rome, but he is referencing that he must obey a higher power than them, but without actually coming right out and saying so!

## LESSON 12: TRAGEDY ENDS IN GLORY

In the Westminster Confession of Faith, one of the proof texts for God's providence is the story of Paul's word from the Lord that no one would be lost and then his springing into action to be a part of the promised rescue. Some have argued that believing that God is in charge of all details great and small will lead to passivity—a let-go-and-let-God type of attitude. But Paul gives us an example of what trusting in God's good providence is meant to look and sound like. He tells everyone to eat, he prevents the sailors from leaving the boat, gives an encouraging speech, and was so effective that the centurion also helped to save everyone's life when the soldiers wanted to kill them all. So God's providence is at work through the actions of his people.

The story of the storm is what is emphasized at the end of the book. Although it is likely that Paul was beheaded in Rome by Nero (according to longstanding church tradition), Luke gives us no indication of how the story will end. There might have been many reasons for that, but surely one key reason is that the story continues as the church continues. And God's people are still weathering storms by faith, still using all their energy to believe in God's promises and to be a part of his kingdom coming all over the world.

# ENDNOTES

1. The items in this exercise are based on those presented by Zacharias Ursinus, *Commentary on the Heidelberg Catechism*, 4th ed., trans. G. W. Williard (Cincinnati, OH: Elm Street Printing, 1888), questions 45–52.

2. Serge, *Sonship*, 3rd ed. (Greensboro, NC: New Growth Press, 2013), 44.

3. Michael Gerson, "Charles Colson Found Freedom in Prison," *Washington Post*, April 22, 2012, www.washingtonpost.com/opinions/finding-freedom-in-prison/2012/04/22/gIQANabcaT_story.html.

4. Encyclopedia Britannica, https://www.britannica.com/art/tragedy-literature/Theory-of-tragedy. Last accessed 04/30/24.